ONE
POT
COOKING

Publications International, Ltd.

CONTENTS

DUTCH OVEN

Spicy Chicken Rigatoni

MAKES 4 SERVINGS

2 tablespoons olive oil

2 cloves garlic, minced

½ teaspoon red pepper flakes

½ teaspoon black pepper

8 ounces boneless skinless chicken breasts, cut into thin strips

1 cup marinara sauce

¾ cup prepared Alfredo sauce

1 package (16 ounces) uncooked rigatoni or penne pasta, cooked until al dente

¾ cup frozen peas, thawed

Grated Parmesan cheese (optional)

1. Heat oil in Dutch oven over medium-high heat. Add garlic, red pepper flakes and black pepper; cook and stir 1 minute. Add chicken; cook and stir 4 minutes or until cooked through.

2. Add marinara sauce and Alfredo sauce; stir until blended. Reduce heat to medium-low; cook 10 minutes, stirring occasionally.

3. Add pasta and peas; stir gently to coat. Cook 2 minutes or until heated through. Sprinkle with cheese, if desired.

Pasta Fagioli

MAKES 8 SERVINGS

2 tablespoons olive oil, divided

1 pound ground beef

1 cup chopped onion

1 cup diced carrots (about 2 medium)

1 cup diced celery (about 2 stalks)

3 cloves garlic, minced

4 cups beef broth

1 can (28 ounces) diced tomatoes

1 can (15 ounces) tomato sauce

1 tablespoon cider vinegar

2 teaspoons sugar

1½ teaspoons dried basil

1¼ teaspoons salt

1 teaspoon dried oregano

¾ teaspoon dried thyme

2 cups uncooked ditalini pasta

1 can (about 15 ounces) dark red kidney beans, rinsed and drained

1 can (about 15 ounces) cannellini beans, rinsed and drained

Grated Romano cheese (optional)

1. Heat 1 tablespoon oil in Dutch oven over medium-high heat. Add beef; cook 5 minutes or until browned, stirring to break up meat. Remove to medium bowl. Drain fat.

2. Add remaining 1 tablespoon oil to Dutch oven; heat over medium-high heat. Add onion, carrots and celery; cook and stir 5 minutes or until vegetables are tender. Add garlic; cook and stir 1 minute. Add cooked beef, broth, tomatoes, tomato sauce, vinegar, sugar, basil, salt, oregano and thyme; bring to a boil. Reduce heat to medium-low; cover and simmer 30 minutes.

3. Add pasta, kidney beans and cannellini beans; cook over medium heat 10 minutes or until pasta is tender, stirring frequently. Top with cheese, if desired.

Tex-Mex Black Bean and Corn Stew

MAKES 4 SERVINGS

1 tablespoon canola
or vegetable oil

1 small onion, chopped

4 cloves garlic, minced

1 teaspoon chili powder

1 teaspoon ground
cumin

½ teaspoon salt

1 can (about 14 ounces)
fire-roasted diced
tomatoes

¾ cup salsa

2 medium zucchini
or yellow squash
(or 1 of each), cut
into ½-inch chunks

1 can (about 15 ounces)
black beans, rinsed
and drained

1 cup frozen corn

½ cup (2 ounces)
shredded Cheddar
or pepper jack
cheese

¼ cup chopped
fresh cilantro
or green onion

1. Heat oil in Dutch oven over medium heat. Add onion; cook and stir 5 minutes. Add garlic, chili powder, cumin and salt; cook and stir 1 minute.

2. Stir in tomatoes, salsa, zucchini, black beans and corn; bring to a boil over high heat. Reduce heat to low; cover and cook 20 minutes or until vegetables are tender. Top with cheese and cilantro.

Ham Jambalaya

MAKES 6 TO 8 SERVINGS

2 tablespoons butter

1 onion, chopped

½ cup thinly sliced celery

½ red bell pepper, diced

2 cloves garlic, minced

1 jar (about 16 ounces) medium salsa

2 cups cubed cooked ham

1 cup uncooked long grain rice

1 cup water

⅔ cup vegetable broth

3 teaspoons prepared horseradish

2 teaspoons honey

¼ to ½ teaspoon hot pepper sauce

1½ pounds medium or large raw shrimp, peeled and deveined

1 tablespoon chopped fresh mint

1. Preheat oven to 350°F.

2. Melt butter in Dutch oven over medium heat. Add onion, celery, bell pepper and garlic; cook and stir 3 minutes or until vegetables are tender. Stir in salsa, ham, rice, water, broth, horseradish, honey and hot pepper sauce; mix well.

3. Cover and bake 40 minutes or until rice is almost tender.

4. Stir in shrimp and mint; bake 10 to 15 minutes or until shrimp are pink and opaque.

Hearty Tuscan Soup

MAKES 6 TO 8 SERVINGS

1 teaspoon olive oil

1 pound bulk mild or
    hot Italian sausage*

1 medium onion,
    chopped

3 cloves garlic, minced

¼ cup all-purpose flour

5 cups chicken broth

1 teaspoon salt

½ teaspoon Italian
    seasoning

3 medium unpeeled
    russet potatoes
    (about 1 pound),
    halved lengthwise
    and thinly sliced

2 cups packed torn
    stemmed kale

1 cup half-and-half or
    whipping cream

*Or use sausage links and
remove from casings.*

1. Heat oil in Dutch oven over medium-high heat. Add sausage; cook until sausage begins to brown, stirring to break up meat. Add onion and garlic; cook about 5 minutes or until onion is softened and sausage is browned, stirring occasionally.

2. Stir in flour until blended. Add broth, salt and Italian seasoning; bring to a boil. Stir in potatoes and kale. Reduce heat to medium-low; cook 15 to 20 minutes or until potatoes are fork-tender.

3. Reduce heat to low; stir in cream. Cook about 5 minutes or until heated through.

Chicken Cassoulet

MAKES 6 SERVINGS

4 slices bacon

¼ cup all-purpose flour

Salt and black pepper

1¾ pounds bone-in chicken pieces

2 chicken sausages (2¼ ounces each), cooked and cut into ¼-inch pieces

1½ cups diced red and green bell peppers

1 medium onion, chopped

2 cloves garlic, minced

1 teaspoon dried thyme

1 to 2 teaspoons olive oil

½ cup dry white wine

2 cans (about 15 ounces each) cannellini or Great Northern beans, rinsed and drained

1. Preheat oven to 350°F.

2. Cook bacon in Dutch oven over medium-high heat until crisp; drain on paper towel-lined plate. Cut into 1-inch pieces.

3. Place flour in shallow bowl; season with salt and black pepper. Coat chicken pieces with flour mixture; shake off excess. Brown chicken in batches in Dutch oven over medium-high heat; remove to plate. Lightly brown sausages in Dutch oven; remove to plate.

4. Add bell peppers, onion, garlic and thyme to Dutch oven; cook and stir over medium heat 5 minutes or until softened, adding oil as needed to prevent sticking. Stir in wine, scraping up browned bits from bottom of pan. Stir in beans; mix well. Top with chicken, sausages and bacon.

5. Cover and bake 40 minutes. Uncover; bake 15 minutes or until chicken is cooked through (165°F).

Vegetarian Chili

MAKES 8 TO 10 SERVINGS

2 tablespoons olive oil

1 onion, finely chopped

2 medium carrots, chopped

1 red bell pepper, chopped

3 tablespoons chili powder

2 tablespoons ground cumin

2 tablespoons tomato paste

2 tablespoons packed dark brown sugar

3 cloves garlic, minced

1 tablespoon dried oregano

1 teaspoon salt

1 can (28 ounces) diced tomatoes

1 can (15 ounces) tomato sauce

1 can (about 15 ounces) small white beans, rinsed and drained

1 can (about 15 ounces) light kidney beans, rinsed and drained

1 can (about 15 ounces) dark kidney beans, rinsed and drained

1 can (about 15 ounces) pinto beans, rinsed and drained

1 cup vegetable broth

1 can (4 ounces) diced mild green chiles

1 ounce unsweetened baking chocolate, chopped

1 tablespoon cider vinegar

1. Heat oil in Dutch oven over medium-high heat. Add onion, carrots and bell pepper; cook 10 minutes or until vegetables are tender, stirring frequently. Add chili powder, cumin, tomato paste, brown sugar, garlic, oregano and salt; cook and stir 1 minute.

2. Stir in tomatoes, tomato sauce, beans, broth, chiles and chocolate; bring to a boil. Reduce heat to medium; cook 20 minutes, stirring occasionally. Stir in vinegar.

DUTCH OVEN

Pozole

MAKES 6 SERVINGS

3 (6-inch) corn tortillas

1 tablespoon vegetable oil

1 large onion, chopped

1 tablespoon minced garlic

1 tablespoon dried oregano

1½ teaspoons ground cumin

2 cans (about 14 ounces each) chicken broth

1½ cups water

1 pound boneless skinless chicken breasts

2 cans (about 15 ounces each) yellow hominy, drained

1 red or green bell pepper, chopped

1 can (4 ounces) diced mild green chiles

1 can (2¼ ounces) sliced black olives, drained

½ cup lightly packed fresh cilantro, coarsely chopped

1. Preheat oven to 450°F.

2. Cut tortillas into ¼-inch-wide strips. Place strips in single layer on baking sheet. Bake 3 to 4 minutes or until crisp. (Do not let strips brown.) Remove to plate to cool.

3. Heat oil in Dutch oven over medium heat. Add onion, garlic, oregano and cumin; cook and stir about 6 minutes or until onion is golden brown, stirring occasionally. Add broth and water; bring to a boil. Stir in chicken. Reduce heat to low; cover and cook 8 minutes or until chicken is no longer pink in center. Remove chicken to plate; set aside until cool enough to handle. Cut into ½-inch pieces.

4. Meanwhile, add hominy, bell pepper, chiles and olives to broth in Dutch oven; bring to a boil over medium-high heat. Reduce heat to medium-low; cover and cook 4 minutes or until bell pepper is crisp-tender. Return chicken to Dutch oven with cilantro; cook just until heated through. Top with toasted tortilla strips.

Beef Stew in Red Wine

MAKES 6 SERVINGS

1½ pounds boneless beef round steak, cut into 1-inch pieces

1½ cups dry red wine

2 teaspoons olive oil

Grated peel of ½ orange

2 cloves garlic, thinly sliced

1 bay leaf

¾ teaspoon salt

½ teaspoon dried thyme

⅛ teaspoon black pepper

8 ounces mushrooms, quartered

8 sun-dried tomatoes, quartered

1 can (about 14 ounces) beef broth

6 unpeeled small red or new potatoes, cut into wedges

1 cup baby carrots

1 cup fresh pearl onions, outer skins removed

1 tablespoon cornstarch mixed with 2 tablespoons water

1. Combine beef, wine, oil, orange peel, garlic, bay leaf, salt, thyme and pepper in large bowl; mix well. Cover and refrigerate at least 2 hours or overnight.

2. Combine beef mixture, mushrooms and sun-dried tomatoes in Dutch oven; add just enough broth to cover. Bring to a boil over high heat. Reduce heat to low; cover and cook 1 hour.

3. Add potatoes, carrots and onions; cover and cook 20 to 25 minutes or until vegetables are tender and meat is no longer pink. Remove meat and vegetables to bowl with slotted spoon. Remove and discard orange peel and bay leaf.

4. Stir cornstarch mixture into sauce in Dutch oven; cook and stir over medium heat until slightly thickened. Return beef and vegetables to sauce; cook until heated through.

Chicken and Gnocchi Soup

MAKES 6 TO 8 SERVINGS

¼ cup (½ stick) butter

1 tablespoon extra virgin olive oil

1 cup finely diced onion

2 stalks celery, finely chopped

2 cloves garlic, minced

¼ cup all-purpose flour

4 cups half-and-half

1 can (about 14 ounces) chicken broth

1 teaspoon salt

½ teaspoon dried thyme

½ teaspoon dried parsley flakes

¼ teaspoon ground nutmeg

1 package (about 16 ounces) gnocchi

1 package (6 ounces) fully cooked chicken strips, chopped *or* 1 cup diced cooked chicken

1 cup shredded carrots

1 cup coarsely chopped fresh spinach

1. Melt butter in Dutch oven over medium heat; add oil. Add onion, celery and garlic; cook about 8 minutes or until vegetables are softened and onion is translucent, stirring occasionally.

2. Whisk in flour; cook and stir about 1 minute. Whisk in half-and-half; cook about 15 minutes or until thickened, stirring occasionally.

3. Whisk in broth, salt, thyme, parsley flakes and nutmeg; cook 10 minutes or until soup is slightly thickened, stirring occasionally. Add gnocchi, chicken, carrots and spinach; cook about 5 minutes or until gnocchi are heated through.

Fettuccine with Vegetable Marinara Sauce

MAKES 4 TO 6 SERVINGS

2 tablespoons extra virgin olive oil

1 medium onion, finely chopped

1 small carrot, finely chopped

1 small stalk celery, finely chopped

2 cloves garlic, finely chopped

1 can (28 ounces) peeled plum tomatoes, undrained

½ cup water

⅓ cup packed chopped fresh basil leaves

Salt and black pepper

1 package (16 ounces) uncooked fettuccine, cooked and drained

Grated Parmesan cheese

1. Heat oil in Dutch oven over medium heat. Add onion, carrot, celery and garlic; cover and cook about 5 minutes or until onion is tender, stirring occasionally.

2. Drain tomatoes, reserving juice. Coarsely crush tomatoes with fingers or wooden spoon. Add tomatoes, reserved juice and water to Dutch oven; bring to a boil over high heat. Reduce heat to medium-low; cook, uncovered, about 45 minutes or until sauce is slightly thickened and reduced, stirring frequently. Stir in basil during last 5 minutes of cooking. Season with salt and pepper.

3. Serve sauce over pasta; top with Parmesan cheese.

Corned Beef and Cabbage

MAKES 8 SERVINGS

3½ to 4 pounds packaged corned beef brisket

3 carrots, peeled and cut into 1½-inch pieces

2 small onions, peeled and quartered

3 stalks celery, cut into 1½-inch pieces

1 bunch fresh parsley

2 large sprigs fresh thyme

1 head green cabbage (about 2 pounds), cut into 8 wedges

1½ pounds unpeeled small red potatoes, quartered

1 cup sour cream

2 tablespoons prepared horseradish

½ teaspoon coarse salt

Chopped fresh parsley (optional)

1. Combine corned beef, carrots, onions and celery in Dutch oven. Tie parsley and thyme together with kitchen string; add to Dutch oven. Add water to cover beef by 1 inch; bring to a boil over high heat. Reduce heat to medium-low; cover and cook about 2½ hours or until beef is almost tender.

2. Add cabbage and potatoes to Dutch oven; cover and cook about 30 minutes or until beef, cabbage and potatoes are tender.

3. Meanwhile, combine sour cream, horseradish and ½ teaspoon salt in medium bowl; mix well. Refrigerate until ready to serve.

4. Remove herbs from Dutch oven and discard. Remove beef to cutting board; let stand 10 minutes. Slice beef across the grain. Arrange on serving platter with vegetables; season vegetables with additional salt to taste. Sprinkle with chopped parsley, if desired; serve with horseradish sauce.

Pasta Campagnolo

MAKES 4 SERVINGS

3 tablespoons olive oil

8 ounces Italian sausage,
casings removed

1 medium onion,
finely chopped

1 red bell pepper, cut
into ¼-inch strips

2 cloves garlic, minced

⅓ cup dry white wine

1 can (28 ounces)
crushed tomatoes

1 can (8 ounces)
tomato sauce

4 tablespoons chopped
fresh basil, divided,
plus addtional for
garnish

½ teaspoon salt

¼ teaspoon black pepper

⅛ teaspoon red pepper
flakes

1 package (16 ounces)
uncooked rigatoni
or penne pasta,
cooked until
al dente

¼ cup grated
Romano cheese

1 package (4 ounces)
goat cheese, cut
crosswise into
8 slices

1. Heat oil in Dutch oven over medium heat. Break sausage into ½-inch pieces; add to Dutch oven. Cook about 5 minutes or until browned, stirring occasionally. Add onion and bell pepper; cook and stir 5 minutes or until vegetables are softened. Add garlic; cook and stir 1 minute.

2. Stir in wine; cook about 5 minutes or until most of liquid has evaporated. Stir in tomatoes, tomato sauce, 2 tablespoons basil, salt, black pepper and red pepper flakes; bring to a boil. Reduce heat to medium-low; cook 20 minutes or until sauce has thickened slightly.

3. Add hot cooked pasta, Romano cheese and remaining 2 tablespoons basil to sauce; stir gently to coat. Cook just until heated through.

4. Top each serving with 1 or 2 slices of goat cheese; garnish with additional basil.

Peppery Sicilian Chicken Soup

MAKES 8 TO 10 SERVINGS

2 tablespoons olive oil

1 onion, chopped

1 green bell pepper, chopped

3 stalks celery, chopped

3 carrots, chopped

3 cloves garlic, minced

1 tablespoon salt

3 containers (32 ounces each) chicken broth

2 pounds boneless skinless chicken breasts

1 can (28 ounces) diced tomatoes

2 baking potatoes, peeled and cut into ¼-inch pieces

1½ teaspoons ground white pepper*

1½ teaspoons ground black pepper

½ cup chopped fresh parsley

8 ounces uncooked ditalini pasta, cooked until al dente

Or substitute additional black pepper for the white pepper.

1. Heat oil in Dutch oven over medium heat. Add onion, bell pepper, celery and carrots. Reduce heat to medium-low; cover and cook 10 to 15 minutes or until vegetables are tender but not browned, stirring occasionally. Stir in garlic and 1 tablespoon salt; cover and cook 5 minutes.

2. Stir in broth, chicken, tomatoes, potatoes, white pepper and black pepper; bring to a boil. Reduce heat to low; cover and cook 1 hour.

3. Remove chicken to plate; set aside until cool enough to handle. Shred chicken and return to Dutch oven with parsley.

4. Stir in pasta; cook until heated through. Taste and add additional salt, if desired.

Espresso-Laced Pot Roast

MAKES 6 TO 8 SERVINGS

2 tablespoons all-purpose flour

1 tablespoon espresso powder

1 tablespoon packed brown sugar

½ teaspoon salt

½ teaspoon black pepper

1 boneless beef chuck pot roast (2 to 2½ pounds)

1½ tablespoons vegetable oil or bacon drippings

1 can (about 14 ounces) beef broth

1 large onion, coarsely chopped

1 pound carrots, cut into 1-inch pieces

6 to 8 red potatoes, peeled and cut into quarters

Chopped fresh parsley (optional)

1. Preheat oven to 350°F. Combine flour, espresso powder, brown sugar, salt and pepper in small bowl; mix well. Rub mixture into all sides of beef.

2. Heat oil in Dutch oven over medium heat. Add beef; cook about 5 minutes or until browned. Turn and cook 3 to 4 minutes or until bottom is browned. Stir in broth and onion.

3. Cover and bake 1 hour. Turn beef; add carrots and potatoes. Cover and bake about 1 hour or until beef and vegetables are fork-tender. Remove beef to cutting board; tent with foil and let stand 10 minutes.

4. Cook vegetables and juices over high heat until liquid is reduced and slightly thickened. Slice beef; return to Dutch oven to coat with sauce. Garnish with parsley.

Sausage Rice Soup

MAKES 4 TO 6 SERVINGS

2 teaspoons olive oil

8 ounces Italian sausage, casings removed

1 small onion, chopped

½ teaspoon fennel seeds

1 tablespoon tomato paste

4 cups chicken broth

1 can (about 14 ounces) whole tomatoes, crushed with hands or chopped, juice reserved

1½ cups water

½ cup uncooked rice

¼ teaspoon salt

⅛ teaspoon black pepper

2 to 3 ounces baby spinach

⅓ cup shredded mozzarella cheese (optional)

1. Heat oil in Dutch oven over medium-high heat. Add sausage; cook about 8 minutes or until browned, breaking up meat into bite-size pieces. Add onion; cook and stir 5 minutes or until softened. Add fennel seeds; cook and stir 30 seconds. Add tomato paste; cook and stir 1 minute.

2. Stir in broth, tomatoes with juice, water, rice, ¼ teaspoon salt and ⅛ teaspoon pepper; bring to a boil. Reduce heat to medium-low; cook about 18 minutes or until rice is tender. Stir in spinach; cook about 3 minutes or until wilted. Season with additional salt and pepper.

3. Sprinkle with cheese, if desired, just before serving.

BAKING DISH

Pizza Chicken Bake

MAKES 4 SERVINGS

3½ cups uncooked
    bowtie pasta,
    cooked until
    al dente

1 tablespoon vegetable
    oil

1 cup sliced mushrooms

1 jar (26 ounces)
    herb-flavored
    pasta sauce

1 teaspoon pizza
    seasoning blend

12 ounces boneless
    skinless chicken
    breasts, cut into
    2-inch pieces

1 cup (4 ounces)
    shredded
    mozzarella cheese

1. Preheat oven to 350°F. Spray 2-quart round baking dish with nonstick cooking spray. Place pasta in prepared dish.

2. Heat oil in large skillet over medium-high heat. Add mushrooms; cook and stir 5 minutes. Add pasta sauce and pizza seasoning; mix well.

3. Pour half of pasta sauce mixture into casserole; stir gently to coat. Top with chicken and remaining pasta sauce mixture.

4. Cover and bake 50 minutes or until chicken is cooked through. Sprinkle with cheese; cover and let stand 5 minutes before serving.

TIP

Serve with grated Parmesan cheese and red pepper flakes so everyone can add their own individual pizza seasonings.

Zucchini with Feta Casserole

MAKES 4 SERVINGS

- 4 medium zucchini
- 1 tablespoon butter
- 2 eggs, beaten
- ½ cup grated Parmesan cheese
- ⅓ cup crumbled feta cheese
- 2 tablespoons chopped fresh parsley
- 1 tablespoon all-purpose flour
- 2 teaspoons chopped fresh marjoram or oregano
- Dash hot pepper sauce
- Salt and black pepper

1. Preheat oven to 375°F. Spray 2-quart baking dish with nonstick cooking spray.

2. Grate zucchini; drain in colander. Melt butter in large skillet over medium heat. Add zucchini; cook and stir until slightly browned.

3. Remove from heat; stir in eggs, Parmesan, feta, parsley, flour, marjoram, hot pepper sauce, salt and black pepper until well blended. Pour into prepared baking dish.

4. Bake 35 minutes or until hot and bubbly.

Ramen Reuben Noodle Bake

MAKES 8 SERVINGS

3 packages (3 ounces each) beef-flavored ramen noodles, cooked 2 minutes with seasoning packets and drained

2 cans (about 14 ounces each) shredded sauerkraut, undrained

1 pound thinly sliced deli corned beef, chopped

¼ cup (½ stick) butter, melted

1½ teaspoons caraway seeds, divided

½ cup Thousand Island dressing

8 slices (6 ounces) Swiss cheese

1. Preheat oven to 350°F. Spray 13×9-inch baking dish with nonstick cooking spray.

2. Combine noodles, sauerkraut with liquid, corned beef, butter and 1 teaspoon caraway seeds in large bowl; stir gently to coat. Transfer to prepared baking dish.

3. Cover and bake 20 minutes or until heated through. Drizzle with dressing; top with cheese and remaining ½ teaspoon caraway seeds. Bake, uncovered, 13 to 15 minutes or until cheese is melted and casserole is bubbly.

Beef, Bean and Pasta Casserole

MAKES 6 SERVINGS

1 **pound ground beef**

1 **medium onion, diced**

2 **cloves garlic, minced**

1 **can (about 15 ounces) cannellini beans, rinsed and drained**

1 **can (about 14 ounces) diced tomatoes, drained**

1 **can (8 ounces) tomato sauce**

2 **teaspoons Italian seasoning**

¾ **teaspoon salt**

¼ **teaspoon black pepper**

3 **cups uncooked whole wheat rigatoni pasta, cooked until al dente**

1 **cup finely shredded Parmesan cheese**

1 **cup (4 ounces) shredded mozzarella cheese**

1. Preheat oven to 350°F. Spray 11×7-inch baking dish with nonstick cooking spray.

2. Cook beef, onion and garlic in large skillet over medium-high heat 6 to 8 minutes or until beef is browned, stirring to break up meat. Drain fat. Add beans, tomatoes, tomato sauce, Italian seasoning, salt and pepper; cook 3 minutes.

3. Remove from heat; stir in pasta and Parmesan. Transfer to prepared baking dish; sprinkle with mozzarella.

4. Bake 20 minutes or until cheese is melted and casserole is bubbly.

VARIATIONS

Any short-shape pasta can be used in this recipe. Red kidney beans can be used in place of the cannellini beans.

Split-Biscuit Chicken Pie

MAKES 4 TO 5 SERVINGS

⅓ cup butter

⅓ cup all-purpose flour

2½ cups whole milk

1 tablespoon chicken bouillon granules

½ teaspoon dried thyme

½ teaspoon black pepper

4 cups diced cooked chicken

2 jars (4 ounces each) diced pimientos

1 cup frozen green peas, thawed

1 package (6 ounces) refrigerated biscuit dough, prepared according to package directions

1. Preheat oven to 350°F. Spray 2-quart or 12×8-inch baking dish with nonstick cooking spray.

2. Melt butter in large skillet over medium heat. Add flour; whisk until smooth. Add milk, bouillon, thyme and pepper; stir until well blended. Cook and stir until thickened. Remove from heat; stir in chicken, pimientos and peas. Transfer to prepared baking dish.

3. Bake 30 minutes. Split biscuits in half; arrange cut sides down over chicken mixture. Bake 3 minutes or until biscuits are heated through.

Creamy Shrimp and Vegetable Casserole

MAKES 4 SERVINGS

1 pound fresh or thawed frozen medium raw shrimp, peeled and deveined

1 can (10¾ ounces) condensed cream of celery soup, undiluted

½ cup sliced fresh or thawed frozen asparagus (1-inch pieces)

½ cup sliced mushrooms

¼ cup diced red bell pepper

¼ cup sliced green onions

1 clove garlic, minced

¾ teaspoon dried thyme

¼ teaspoon black pepper

Hot cooked rice or orzo (optional)

1. Preheat oven to 375°F. Spray 2-quart baking dish with nonstick cooking spray.

2. Combine shrimp, soup, asparagus, mushrooms, bell pepper, green onions, garlic, thyme and black pepper in large bowl; mix well. Transfer to prepared baking dish.

3. Cover and bake 30 minutes. Serve over rice, if desired.

Chipotle Turkey Strata

MAKES 6 SERVINGS

6 to 8 Italian bread slices (½ inch thick)

2 tablespoons chipotle sauce*

2 cups chopped cooked turkey

1½ cups (6 ounces) shredded Cheddar cheese, divided

5 eggs

2½ cups milk

½ teaspoon salt

¼ teaspoon black pepper

If chipotle sauce is unavailable, substitute 1 tablespoon tomato sauce blended with 1 tablespoon adobo sauce from canned chipotle chiles in adobo.

1. Preheat oven to 325°F. Spray 9-inch square baking dish with nonstick cooking spray.

2. Arrange 3 to 4 bread slices to cover bottom of dish, cutting bread to fit, if necessary. Spread chipotle sauce over bread. Top with turkey; sprinkle with 1 cup cheese. Cover with remaining 3 to 4 bread slices.

3. Beat eggs, milk, salt and pepper in medium bowl until blended. Pour over bread; press down firmly so bread absorbs liquid. Top with remaining ½ cup cheese.

4. Bake 60 to 70 minutes or until set and golden brown. Let stand 10 to 15 minutes before cutting.

Sausage and Polenta Casserole

MAKES 4 SERVINGS

1 tablespoon olive oil

1 cup chopped
   mushrooms

1 red bell pepper, diced

1 onion, diced

1 pound bulk Italian
   sausage

1 jar (28 to 30 ounces)
   pasta sauce

1 roll (16 to 18 ounces)
   polenta

¼ cup shredded
   Parmesan cheese

1. Preheat oven to 350°F. Spray 8-inch square baking dish with nonstick cooking spray.

2. Heat oil in large skillet over medium heat. Add mushrooms, bell pepper and onion; cook and stir 5 minutes or until vegetables are tender. Add sausage; cook and stir until sausage is browned, breaking meat into small pieces with spoon. Drain fat. Stir in pasta sauce; cook 5 minutes, stirring occasionally.

3. Cut polenta crosswise into 9 slices; arrange in prepared baking dish. Top with sausage mixture.

4. Bake 15 minutes or until heated through. Sprinkle with cheese.

Bowtie Zucchini

MAKES 8 SERVINGS

¼ cup olive oil

1 cup chopped onion

2 cloves garlic, minced

5 small zucchini, cut into thin strips

⅔ cup whipping cream

1 package (16 ounces) uncooked bowtie pasta, cooked until al dente

¼ cup grated Parmesan cheese

Salt and black pepper

1. Preheat oven to 350°F. Spray 2-quart baking dish with nonstick cooking spray.

2. Heat oil in large skillet over medium-high heat. Add onion and garlic; cook and stir 3 minutes or until onion is translucent. Add zucchini; cook and stir until tender.

3. Add cream; cook and stir until thickened. Add pasta and cheese to skillet; season with salt and pepper. Transfer to prepared baking dish.

4. Cover and bake 15 minutes or until heated through.

Taco Salad Casserole

MAKES 6 TO 8 SERVINGS

1 pound ground beef

1 cup chopped onion

1 can (15 ounces) chili
with beans

1 can (about 14 ounces)
diced tomatoes

1 can (4 ounces)
diced green chilies

1 package (about
1 ounce) taco
seasoning mix

1 bag (12 ounces)
nacho-flavor tortilla
chips, crushed

2 cups (8 ounces)
shredded Cheddar
cheese

2 cups (8 ounces)
shredded
mozzarella cheese

3 to 4 cups shredded
lettuce

1 jar (8 ounces)
prepared
taco sauce

½ cup sour cream

1. Preheat oven to 350°F.

2. Cook and stir beef and onion in large skillet over medium
heat until beef is no longer pink, stirring to break up meat.
Drain fat. Add chili with beans, tomatoes, green chiles
and taco seasoning mix; cook 5 minutes or until heated
through, stirring occasionally.

3. Place half of crushed tortilla chips in 2½-quart baking
dish. Pour beef mixture over chips; top with Cheddar,
mozzarella and remaining chips.

4. Bake 30 to 40 minutes or until hot and bubbly. Serve over
lettuce; top with taco sauce and sour cream.

Spinach-Cheese Pasta Casserole

MAKES 6 TO 8 SERVINGS

2 eggs

1 cup ricotta cheese

1 package (10 ounces) frozen chopped spinach, thawed and squeezed dry

8 ounces uncooked shell pasta, cooked until al dente

1 jar (26 ounces) marinara sauce

1 teaspoon salt

1 cup (4 ounces) shredded mozzarella cheese

¼ cup grated Parmesan cheese

1. Preheat oven to 350°F. Spray 1½-quart baking dish with nonstick cooking spray.

2. Beat eggs in large bowl. Add ricotta and spinach; stir until blended. Add pasta, marinara sauce and salt; stir gently to coat. Transfer to prepared baking dish; sprinkle with mozzarella and Parmesan.

3. Cover and bake 30 minutes. Uncover; bake 15 minutes or until hot and bubbly.

Sausage, Potato and Apple Bake

MAKES 6 SERVINGS

3 tablespoons packed brown sugar

1 tablespoon dried thyme

1 tablespoon dried oregano

¼ cup dry white wine or apple cider

2 tablespoons cider vinegar

2 sweet potatoes (1½ to 2 pounds), peeled and spiraled or cut into strips

2 apples, such as Fuji or McIntosh, peeled and spiraled or cut into strips

1 red bell pepper, spiraled or cut into strips

1 yellow bell pepper, spiraled or cut into strips

1 white onion, spiraled or cut into strips

½ cup golden raisins

1½ pounds smoked sausage, such as kielbasa or Polish sausage, cut diagonally into ¼-inch slices

1. Preheat oven to 450°F. Spray 2-quart or 13×9-inch baking dish with nonstick cooking spray.

2. Combine brown sugar, thyme and oregano in large bowl; mix well. Stir in white wine and vinegar until brown sugar is dissolved.

3. Add sweet potatoes, apples, bell peppers, onion and raisins to brown sugar mixture; toss to coat. Transfer vegetables to prepared baking dish with tongs or slotted spoon. Stir in sausage; drizzle with remaining brown sugar mixture.

4. Bake 20 minutes or until vegetables are tender.

Tuna Tomato Casserole

MAKES 6 SERVINGS

2 cans (6 ounces each) tuna, drained and flaked

1 cup mayonnaise

1 onion, finely chopped

½ teaspoon salt

¼ teaspoon black pepper

1 package (12 ounces) uncooked wide egg noodles, cooked until al dente

8 to 10 plum tomatoes, sliced ¼ inch thick

1 cup (4 ounces) shredded Cheddar or mozzarella cheese

1. Preheat oven to 375°F. Spray 13×9-inch baking dish with nonstick cooking spray.

2. Combine tuna, mayonnaise, onion, salt and pepper in large bowl; mix well. Add noodles; stir gently to coat.

3. Layer half of noodle mixture, half of tomatoes and half of cheese in prepared baking dish; press down slightly. Repeat layers.

4. Bake 20 minutes or until cheese is melted and casserole is heated through.

Spinach Artichoke Gratin

MAKES 6 SERVINGS

2 cups cottage cheese

2 eggs

5 tablespoons grated
  Parmesan cheese,
  divided

1 tablespoon lemon
  juice

¼ teaspoon salt

⅛ teaspoon black
  pepper

⅛ teaspoon ground
  nutmeg

2 packages (10 ounces
  each) frozen
  chopped spinach,
  thawed

⅓ cup thinly sliced
  green onions

1 package (10 ounces)
  frozen artichoke
  hearts, thawed and
  halved

1. Preheat oven to 375°F. Spray 1½-quart baking dish with nonstick cooking spray.

2. Combine cottage cheese, eggs, 3 tablespoons Parmesan, lemon juice, salt, pepper and nutmeg in food processor or blender; process until smooth.

3. Squeeze moisture from spinach. Combine spinach, cottage cheese mixture and green onions in large bowl; mix well. Spread half of mixture in prepared baking dish.

4. Pat artichokes dry with paper towels; arrange in single layer over spinach mixture. Sprinkle with remaining 2 tablespoons Parmesan; top with remaining spinach mixture.

5. Cover and bake 25 minutes.

Seafood Newburg Casserole

MAKES 6 SERVINGS

1 can (10¾ ounces)
   condensed cream
   of shrimp soup,
   undiluted

½ cup half-and-half

1 tablespoon dry sherry

¼ teaspoon ground
   red pepper

3 cups cooked rice

2 cans (6 ounces each)
   lump crabmeat,
   drained

4 ounces medium raw
   shrimp, peeled
   and deveined

4 ounces bay scallops,
   rinsed and patted
   dry

1 jar (4 ounces)
   pimientos, drained
   and chopped

¼ cup finely chopped
   fresh parsley

1. Preheat oven to 350°F. Spray 2½-quart baking dish with nonstick cooking spray.

2. Combine soup, half-and-half, sherry and red pepper in large bowl; mix well. Pick out and discard any shell or cartilage from crabmeat. Add rice, crabmeat, shrimp, scallops and pimientos to soup mixture; mix well. Transfer to prepared baking dish.

3. Cover and bake 25 minutes or until shrimp and scallops are opaque. Sprinkle with parsley.

SKILLET

Chicken Sausage and Two-Grain Skillet

MAKES 4 SERVINGS

1 tablespoon olive oil

1 package (12 ounces) fully cooked chicken apple sausage links, cut into ½-inch slices

1 can (about 14 ounces) chicken broth

1 cup instant brown rice

½ cup uncooked quinoa

1 red bell pepper, cut into thin strips

1 stalk celery, sliced diagonally

1½ teaspoons curry powder *or* 1 teaspoon ground turmeric

½ cup thawed frozen peas

¼ cup finely chopped green onion (optional)

1. Heat oil in large skillet over medium-high heat. Add sausage; cook 3 minutes or until edges are browned, stirring occasionally.

2. Stir in broth, rice, quinoa, bell pepper, celery and curry powder; bring to a boil. Reduce heat to low, cover and cook 12 minutes or until liquid is absorbed.

3. Remove from heat; stir in peas. Let stand 5 minutes before serving. Sprinkle with green onions, if desired.

Jambalaya Pasta

MAKES 4 SERVINGS

1 pound boneless skinless chicken breasts, cut into 1-inch pieces

2 tablespoons plus 1 teaspoon Cajun spice blend, divided

1 tablespoon vegetable oil

8 ounces bell peppers (red, yellow, green or a combination), cut into ¼-inch strips

½ medium red onion, cut into ¼-inch strips

6 ounces medium raw shrimp, peeled and deveined

2 cloves garlic, minced

1 teaspoon salt

¼ teaspoon black pepper

1½ pounds plum tomatoes (about 6), cut into ½-inch pieces

1 cup chicken broth

1 package (16 ounces) fresh or dried linguini, cooked until al dente

Chopped fresh parsley

1. Combine chicken and 2 tablespoons Cajun seasoning in medium bowl; toss to coat. Heat oil in large skillet over medium-high heat. Add chicken; cook and stir 3 minutes.

2. Add bell peppers and onion; cook and stir 3 minutes. Add shrimp, garlic, remaining 1 teaspoon Cajun seasoning, salt and black pepper; cook and stir 1 minute.

3. Stir in tomatoes and broth; bring to a boil. Reduce heat to medium-low; cook 3 minutes or until shrimp are pink and opaque. Serve over hot pasta; sprinkle with parsley.

Mexican Turkey Skillet

MAKES 4 SERVINGS

1 tablespoon vegetable oil

12 ounces ground turkey

1 can (about 14 ounces) stewed tomatoes

½ (16-ounce) package frozen bell pepper stir-fry blend, thawed

¾ teaspoon ground cumin

½ teaspoon salt

½ cup (2 ounces) finely shredded sharp Cheddar cheese

2 ounces tortilla chips, broken

1. Heat oil in large skillet over medium heat. Add turkey; cook until no longer pink, stirring to break up meat.

2. Stir in tomatoes, bell peppers, cumin and salt; bring to a boil. Reduce heat to low; cover and cook 20 minutes or until vegetables are tender.

3. Sprinkle with cheese and chips.

Southwestern Chicken and Rice Skillet

MAKES 4 SERVINGS

1 teaspoon chili powder

1 teaspoon ground cumin

4 boneless skinless chicken breast halves (4 to 6 ounces each), pounded to ½-inch thickness

1 tablespoon vegetable oil

2 cloves garlic, minced

2 cups diced zucchini or yellow squash

½ cup salsa

1 package (8½ ounces) cooked brown rice

½ cup (2 ounces) shredded Mexican cheese blend

¼ cup chopped fresh cilantro

1. Combine chili powder and cumin in small bowl; sprinkle over both sides of chicken. Heat oil in large nonstick skillet over medium-high heat. Add chicken; cook 3 to 4 minutes per side or until chicken is no longer pink in center. Remove to plate.

2. Add garlic to skillet; cook and stir 30 seconds. Add zucchini; cook and stir 3 minutes. Stir in salsa; cook 2 minutes or until zucchini is crisp-tender. Stir in rice; cook until heated through.

3. Return chicken to skillet; top with cheese and cilantro. Cover and cook about 3 minutes or until cheese is melted and chicken is heated through.

Pork with Apples, Fennel and Cabbage

MAKES 4 SERVINGS

1 cup apple juice, divided, plus additional as needed

2 tablespoons balsamic vinegar

½ teaspoon caraway seeds

½ teaspoon dried thyme

4 boneless pork chops (4 to 6 ounces each)

¼ teaspoon salt

¼ teaspoon black pepper

1 tablespoon vegetable oil

3 cups sliced green cabbage

1 medium bulb fennel, cut into ¼-inch slices

1 small onion, cut into ¼-inch rings

1 large apple, thinly sliced

1 tablespoon cornstarch

1. Combine ⅔ cup apple juice, vinegar, caraway seeds and thyme in small bowl; mix well.

2. Sprinkle pork with salt and pepper. Heat oil in large nonstick skillet over medium-high heat. Add pork; cook 2 to 3 minutes per side or until lightly browned. Remove to plate.

3. Add cabbage, fennel, onion and apple juice mixture to skillet. Reduce heat to medium-low; cover and cook 15 minutes, stirring occasionally.

4. Return pork chops and any accumulated juices to skillet. Add apple; cover and cook 5 minutes or until pork is barely pink in center. Remove pork, apple and vegetables to plate with slotted spoon; cover to keep warm. Measure juices from skillet; add additional apple juice if necessary to equal 1 cup. Return to skillet.

5. Stir remaining ⅓ cup apple juice into cornstarch in small bowl until smooth. Add to skillet; cook and stir over medium heat until sauce boils and thickens. Serve over pork and vegetables.

Chicken Fried Rice

MAKES 4 SERVINGS

2 tablespoons vegetable oil, divided

12 ounces boneless skinless chicken breasts, cut into ½-inch pieces

Salt and black pepper

2 tablespoons butter

2 cloves garlic, minced

½ sweet onion, diced

1 medium carrot, diced

2 green onions, thinly sliced

3 eggs

4 cups cooked white rice*

3 tablespoons soy sauce

2 tablespoons sesame seeds

For rice, cook 1½ cups white rice according to package directions without oil or butter. Spread hot rice on large rimmed baking sheet; cool to room temperature. Refrigerate several hours or overnight. Measure 4 cups.

1. Heat 1 tablespoon oil in large skillet over medium-high heat. Add chicken; season with salt and pepper. Cook and stir 5 to 6 minutes or until cooked through. Add butter and garlic; cook and stir 1 minute or until butter is melted. Remove to small bowl.

2. Add sweet onion, carrots and green onions to skillet; cook and stir over high heat 3 minutes or until vegetables are softened. Add to bowl with chicken.

3. Heat remaining 1 tablespoon oil in same skillet. Crack eggs into skillet; cook and stir 45 seconds or until eggs are scrambled but still moist.

4. Add chicken and vegetable mixture, rice, soy sauce and sesame seeds to skillet; cook and stir 2 minutes or until well blended and heated through. Season with additional salt and pepper.

Tuscan Lamb Skillet

MAKES 4 SERVINGS

8 lamb rib chops
    (1½ pounds total),
    1 inch thick

2 teaspoons olive oil

3 teaspoons minced
    garlic

1 can (19 ounces)
    cannellini beans,
    rinsed and drained

1 can (about 14 ounces)
    Italian-style
    tomatoes, broken
    up, undrained

1 tablespoon balsamic
    vinegar

2 teaspoons minced
    fresh rosemary

    Additional fresh
    rosemary (optional)

1. Trim fat from lamb chops. Heat oil in large skillet over medium heat. Add lamb; cook about 4 minutes per side or until 160°F for medium doneness. Remove lamb to plate; tent with foil.

2. Add garlic to drippings in skillet; cook and stir 1 minute. Stir in beans, tomatoes with juice, vinegar and minced rosemary; bring to a boil. Reduce heat to medium-low; cook 5 minutes, stirring occasionally.

3. Divide bean mixture among four plates; top with lamb. Garnish with additional rosemary.

Prosciutto-Wrapped Snapper

MAKES 4 SERVINGS

1 tablespoon plus 1 teaspoon olive oil, divided

2 cloves garlic, minced

4 skinless red snapper or halibut fillets (6 to 7 ounces each)

½ teaspoon salt

½ teaspoon black pepper

8 large fresh sage leaves

8 thin slices prosciutto (4 ounces)

¼ cup dry marsala wine

1. Preheat oven to 400°F.

2. Combine 1 tablespoon oil and garlic in small bowl; brush over fish. Sprinkle with salt and pepper. Place 2 sage leaves on each fillet. Wrap 2 slices prosciutto around fish to enclose sage leaves; tuck in ends of prosciutto.

3. Heat remaining 1 teaspoon oil in large ovenproof nonstick skillet over medium-high heat. Add fish, sage side down; cook 3 to 4 minutes or until prosciutto is crisp. Carefully turn fish; place skillet in oven.

4. Bake 8 to 10 minutes or until center of fish is opaque. Remove to serving plates; cover to keep warm.

5. Pour wine into skillet, scraping up browned bits from bottom of skillet. Cook and stir over medium-high heat 2 to 3 minutes or until sauce has reduced by half. Drizzle over fish.

Skillet Lasagna with Vegetables

MAKES 6 SERVINGS

8 ounces hot Italian turkey sausage, casings removed

8 ounces ground turkey

2 stalks celery, sliced

⅓ cup chopped onion

2 cups marinara sauce

1⅓ cups water

4 ounces uncooked bowtie pasta

1 medium zucchini, halved lengthwise, then cut crosswise into ½-inch slices

¾ cup chopped green or yellow bell pepper

½ cup (2 ounces) shredded mozzarella cheese

½ cup ricotta cheese

2 tablespoons grated Parmesan cheese

1. Heat large skillet over medium-high heat. Add sausage, ground turkey, celery and onion; cook and stir 6 to 8 minutes or until turkey is no longer pink. Stir in marinara sauce and water; bring to a boil. Stir in pasta. Reduce heat to medium-low; cover and cook 12 minutes.

2. Stir in zucchini and bell pepper; cover and cook 2 minutes. Uncover; cook 4 to 6 minutes or until vegetables are crisp-tender.

3. Sprinkle with mozzarella. Combine ricotta and Parmesan in small bowl; mix well. Drop by rounded teaspoonfuls over pasta mixture in skillet. Remove from heat; cover and let stand 10 minutes.

Aussie Chicken

MAKES 4 SERVINGS

½ cup honey

½ cup Dijon mustard

2 tablespoons vegetable oil, divided

1 teaspoon lemon juice

4 boneless skinless chicken breasts (about 6 ounces each)

Salt and black pepper

1 tablespoon butter

2 cups sliced mushrooms

4 slices bacon, cooked

½ cup (2 ounces) shredded Cheddar cheese

½ cup (2 ounces) shredded Monterey Jack cheese

Chopped fresh parsley

1. Whisk honey, mustard, 1 tablespoon oil and lemon juice in medium bowl until well blended. Remove half of marinade mixture to use as sauce; cover and refrigerate until ready to serve.

2. Place chicken in large resealable food storage bag. Pour remaining half of marinade over chicken; seal bag and turn to coat. Refrigerate at least 2 hours.

3. Preheat oven to 375°F. Remove chicken from marinade; discard marinade. Heat remaining 1 tablespoon oil in large ovenproof skillet over medium-high heat. Add chicken; cook 3 to 4 minutes per side or until golden brown. (Chicken will not be cooked through.) Remove chicken to plate; sprinkle with salt and pepper.

4. Heat butter in same skillet over medium-high heat. Add mushrooms; cook 8 minutes or until mushrooms begin to brown, stirring occasionally and scraping up browned bits from bottom of skillet. Season with salt and pepper. Return chicken to skillet; spoon mushrooms over chicken. Top with bacon; sprinkle with Cheddar and Monterey Jack.

5. Bake 8 to 10 minutes or until chicken is no longer pink in center and cheeses are melted. Sprinkle with parsley; serve with reserved honey-mustard mixture.

Pork and Corn Bread Stuffing Skillet

MAKES 4 SERVINGS

½ **teaspoon paprika**

¼ **teaspoon salt**

¼ **teaspoon garlic powder**

¼ **teaspoon black pepper**

4 **bone-in pork chops (6 to 8 ounces each)**

2 **tablespoons butter**

1½ **cups chopped onions**

¾ **cup thinly sliced celery**

¾ **cup matchstick carrots***

¼ **cup chopped fresh Italian parsley**

1 **can (about 14 ounces) chicken broth**

4 **cups corn bread stuffing mix**

*Matchstick carrots (sometimes called shredded carrots) can be found near other prepared vegetables in supermarket produce section.

1. Preheat oven to 350°F.

2. Combine paprika, salt, garlic powder and pepper in small bowl; sprinkle over both sides of pork chops.

3. Melt butter in large ovenproof skillet over medium-high heat. Add pork; cook 2 minutes per side or just until browned. Remove to plate.

4. Add onions, celery, carrots and parsley to skillet; cook and stir 4 minutes or until onions are translucent. Stir in broth; bring to a boil. Remove from heat; add stuffing mix and fluff with fork. Arrange pork on top of stuffing mixture.

5. Cover and bake 25 minutes or until pork is barely pink in center.

Vegetable Quinoa Frittata

MAKES 6 SERVINGS

1 tablespoon olive oil

1 cup diced onion

1 cup small broccoli florets

¾ cup finely chopped red bell pepper

2 cloves garlic, minced

1¼ teaspoons coarse salt

¼ teaspoon black pepper

1½ cups cooked quinoa

¼ cup sun-dried tomatoes, chopped

8 eggs, lightly beaten

¼ cup grated Parmesan cheese

1. Preheat oven to 400°F.

2. Heat oil in large ovenproof skillet over medium-high heat. Add onion and broccoli; cook and stir 4 minutes, Add bell pepper; cook and stir 2 minutes. Add garlic, salt and black pepper; cook and stir 30 seconds. Stir in quinoa and sun-dried tomatoes.

3. Stir in eggs; cook until softly scrambled. Sprinkle with cheese.

4. Bake about 7 minutes or until eggs are set. Let stand 5 minutes before cutting into wedges.

Chicken Marsala

MAKES 4 SERVINGS

4 boneless skinless
  chicken breasts
  (6 to 8 ounces each)

½ cup all-purpose flour

1 teaspoon coarse salt

¼ teaspoon black
  pepper

2 tablespoons olive oil

3 tablespoons butter,
  divided

2 cups (16 ounces)
  sliced mushrooms

1 shallot, minced (about
  2 tablespoons)

1 clove garlic, minced

1 cup dry Marsala wine

½ cup chicken broth

  Finely chopped
  fresh parsley

1. Pound chicken to ¼-inch thickness between two sheets of plastic wrap. Combine flour, salt and pepper in shallow dish; mix well. Coat both sides of chicken with flour mixture, shaking off excess.

2. Heat oil and 1 tablespoon butter in large skillet over medium-high heat. Add chicken in single layer; cook about 4 minutes per side or until golden brown. Remove to plate; tent with foil.

3. Add 1 tablespoon butter, mushrooms and shallot to skillet; cook about 10 minutes or until mushrooms are deep golden brown, stirring occasionally. Add garlic; cook and stir 1 minute. Stir in Marsala and broth; cook 2 minutes, scraping up browned bits from bottom of skillet. Stir in remaining 1 tablespoon butter until melted.

4. Return chicken to skillet; turn to coat with sauce. Cook 2 minutes or until heated through. Sprinkle with parsley.

Fish Tacos with Cilantro Cream Sauce

MAKES 4 SERVINGS

½ cup sour cream

¼ cup chopped fresh cilantro

1¼ teaspoons ground cumin, divided

1 pound skinless tilapia, mahimahi or other firm white fish fillets

1 teaspoon chipotle hot pepper sauce, divided

1 teaspoon garlic salt

1 tablespoon canola or vegetable oil

1 red bell pepper, cut into strips

1 green bell pepper, cut into strips

8 corn tortillas, warmed

4 limes, cut into wedges

1. For sauce, combine sour cream, cilantro and ¼ teaspoon cumin in small bowl; mix well. Refrigerate until ready to serve.

2. Cut fish into 1-inch pieces; place in medium bowl. Add remaining 1 teaspoon cumin, ½ teaspoon hot pepper sauce and garlic salt; toss to coat.

3. Heat oil in large nonstick skillet over medium heat. Add fish; cook about 2 minutes per side or until center is opaque. Remove to plate. Add bell peppers to skillet; cook and stir 6 to 8 minutes or until tender.

4. Return fish to skillet with remaining ½ teaspoon hot pepper sauce; cook and stir just until heated through. Serve mixture in tortillas with sauce and lime wedges.

Vegetable Penne Italiano

MAKES 4 SERVINGS

1 tablespoon olive oil

1 red bell pepper, cut into ½-inch pieces

1 green bell pepper, cut into ½-inch pieces

1 medium sweet onion, halved and thinly sliced

3 cloves garlic, minced

2 tablespoons tomato paste

2 teaspoons salt

1 teaspoon sugar

1 teaspoon Italian seasoning

¼ teaspoon black pepper

1 can (28 ounces) Italian plum tomatoes, chopped, juice reserved

8 ounces uncooked penne pasta, cooked until al dente

Grated Parmesan cheese

Chopped fresh basil

1. Heat oil in large skillet over medium-high heat. Add bell peppers, onion and garlic; cook and stir 8 minutes or until vegetables are crisp-tender.

2. Add tomato paste, salt, sugar, Italian seasoning and black pepper; cook and stir 1 minute. Stir in tomatoes with juice. Reduce heat to medium-low; cook 15 minutes or until vegetables are tender and sauce is thickened.

3. Add pasta to sauce; stir gently to coat. Cook just until heated through. Top with cheese and basil.

Chicken Fajita Roll-Ups

MAKES 4 SERVINGS

1 cup ranch dressing

1 teaspoon chili powder

2 tablespoons vegetable oil, divided

2 teaspoons lime juice

2 teaspoons fajita seasoning mix

½ teaspoon chipotle chili powder

¼ teaspoon salt

4 boneless skinless chicken breasts (about 6 ounces each)

4 fajita-size flour tortillas (8 to 9 inches)

1 cup (4 ounces) shredded Cheddar cheese

1 cup (4 ounces) shredded Monterey Jack cheese

3 cups shredded lettuce

1 cup pico de gallo

1. Combine ranch dressing and chili powder in small bowl; mix well. Refrigerate until ready to serve.

2. Combine 1 tablespoon oil, lime juice, fajita seasoning mix, chipotle chili powder and salt in small bowl; mix well. Coat both sides of chicken with spice mixture.

3. Heat remaining 1 tablespoon oil in large nonstick skillet over medium-high heat. Add chicken; cook about 5 minutes per side or until cooked through. Remove to plate; let stand 10 minutes before slicing. Cut chicken breasts in half lengthwise, then cut crosswise into ½-inch strips.

4. Wipe out skillet with paper towel. Place 1 tortilla in skillet; sprinkle ¼ cup Cheddar and ¼ cup Monterey Jack evenly over entire surface. Heat over medium heat until cheeses are melted. Remove tortilla to clean work surface or cutting board.

5. Sprinkle ¾ cup shredded lettuce down center of one tortilla; top with ¼ cup pico de gallo and one fourth of chicken. Fold bottom of tortilla up over filling, then fold in sides and roll up. Cut in half diagonally. Repeat with remaining tortillas, cheese and fillings. Serve with ranch dipping sauce.

SHEET PAN

Roast Chicken and Potatoes Catalan

MAKES 4 SERVINGS

2 tablespoons olive oil

2 tablespoons lemon juice

1 teaspoon dried thyme

½ teaspoon salt

¼ teaspoon ground red pepper

¼ teaspoon ground saffron *or* ½ teaspoon crushed saffron threads or turmeric

2 large baking potatoes (about 1½ pounds), cut into 1½-inch pieces

4 skinless bone-in chicken breasts (about 8 ounces each)

1 cup sliced red bell pepper

1 cup frozen peas, thawed

Lemon wedges

1. Preheat oven to 400°F. Spray baking sheet with nonstick cooking spray.

2. Combine oil, lemon juice, thyme, salt, ground red pepper and saffron in large bowl; mix well. Add potatoes; toss to coat.

3. Arrange potatoes in single layer around edges of baking sheet. Place chicken in center of baking sheet; brush both sides of chicken with remaining oil mixture in bowl.

4. Roast 20 minutes. Turn potatoes; baste chicken with pan juices. Add bell pepper; continue roasting 20 minutes or until chicken is no longer pink in center, juices run clear and potatoes are browned. Stir peas into potato mixture; roast 5 minutes or until heated through. Garnish with lemon wedges.

Restaurant-Style Baby Back Ribs

MAKES 4 SERVINGS

1¼ cups water

1 cup white vinegar

⅔ cup packed dark brown sugar

½ cup tomato paste

1 tablespoon yellow mustard

1½ teaspoons salt

1 teaspoon liquid smoke

1 teaspoon onion powder

½ teaspoon garlic powder

½ teaspoon paprika

2 racks pork baby back ribs (3½ to 4 pounds total)

1. Combine water, vinegar, brown sugar, tomato paste, mustard, salt, liquid smoke, onion powder, garlic powder and paprika in medium saucepan; bring to a boil over medium heat. Reduce heat to medium-low; cook 30 minutes or until sauce thickens, stirring occasionally.

2. Preheat oven to 300°F. Place each rack of ribs on large sheet of heavy-duty foil. Brush some of sauce over ribs, covering completely. Fold down edges of foil tightly to seal and create packet; arrange packets on baking sheet, seam sides up.

3. Bake 2 hours. Preheat broiler. Carefully drain off excess liquid from rib packets.

4. Brush ribs with sauce; broil about 5 minutes per side or until beginning to char, brushing with sauce once or twice during cooking. Serve with remaining sauce.

Parmesan-Crusted Tilapia

MAKES 4 SERVINGS

⅔ cup plus 3 tablespoons grated Parmesan cheese, divided

⅔ cup panko bread crumbs

⅓ cup prepared Alfredo sauce (refrigerated or jarred)

1½ teaspoons dried parsley flakes

4 tilapia fillets (6 ounces each)

Shaved Parmesan cheese (optional)

Minced fresh parsley (optional)

1. Preheat oven to 425°F. Line baking sheet with foil; spray foil with nonstick cooking spray.

2. Combine ⅔ cup grated cheese and panko in medium bowl; mix well. Combine Alfredo sauce, remaining 3 tablespoons grated cheese and parsley flakes in small bowl; mix well. Spread sauce mixture over top of fish, coating in thick even layer. Top with panko mixture, pressing in gently to adhere. Place fish on prepared baking sheet.

3. Bake on top rack of oven about 15 minutes or until crust is golden brown and fish begins to flake when tested with fork. Garnish with shaved Parmesan and fresh parsley.

Mounded Mini Meat Loaves

MAKES 4 SERVINGS

1 can (8 ounces) tomato sauce, divided

¼ cup ketchup

2 teaspoons Worcestershire sauce, divided

1 pound ground beef

1 cup cooked and cooled quinoa, any variety*

1 cup chopped bell green pepper

½ cup finely chopped onion

2 eggs, beaten

¾ teaspoon salt

½ teaspoon black pepper

Cook ⅓ cup uncooked quinoa with ⅔ cup water according to package directions. Place cooked quinoa in fine-mesh sieve; run under cold running water to cool quickly. Drain well.

1. Preheat oven to 350°F. Generously spray baking sheet with nonstick cooking spray or line with parchment paper.

2. Combine ¼ cup tomato sauce, ketchup and ½ teaspoon Worcestershire sauce in small bowl; mix well. Set aside for topping.

3. Combine remaining tomato sauce, 1½ teaspoons Worcestershire sauce, beef, quinoa, bell pepper, onion, eggs, salt and black pepper in medium bowl; mix well. Divide mixture into four portions; shape each into individual meat loaf (about 3 inches wide, 5 inches long and 1 inch high) on prepared baking sheet. Mixture will be slightly moist.

4. Bake 35 minutes or until meat loaves are 165°F. Spoon reserved ketchup mixture over tops and sides of meat loaves; bake 10 minutes.

Honey Lemon Garlic Chicken

MAKES 4 SERVINGS

2 lemons, divided

2 tablespoons butter, melted

2 tablespoons honey

3 cloves garlic, chopped

2 sprigs fresh rosemary, leaves removed from stems

1 teaspoon coarse salt

½ teaspoon black pepper

3 pounds chicken (4 bone-in skin-on chicken thighs and 4 drumsticks)

1¼ pounds unpeeled small potatoes, cut into halves or quarters

1. Preheat oven to 375°F. Grate peel and squeeze juice from 1 lemon. Cut remaining lemon into slices.

2. Combine lemon peel, lemon juice, butter, honey, garlic, rosemary leaves, salt and pepper in small bowl; mix well.

3. Combine chicken, potatoes and lemon slices on baking sheet. Pour butter mixture over chicken and potatoes; toss to coat. Spread in single layer.

4. Bake about 1 hour or until potatoes are tender and chicken is cooked through (165°F). Cover loosely with foil if chicken skin is becoming too dark.

Mexican Pizza

MAKES 8 SERVINGS

1 package (about 14 ounces) refrigerated pizza dough

1 cup chunky salsa

1 teaspoon ground cumin

1 cup canned black beans, rinsed and drained

1 cup frozen corn, thawed

½ cup sliced green onions

1½ cups (6 ounces) shredded Mexican cheese blend

½ cup chopped fresh cilantro (optional)

1. Preheat oven to 425°F. Spray baking sheet with nonstick cooking spray. Unroll dough on baking sheet; press dough to edges of pan.

2. Bake 8 minutes. Combine salsa and cumin in small bowl; spread over partially baked crust. Top with beans, corn and green onions. Bake 8 minutes or until crust is deep golden brown.

3. Sprinkle with cheese; bake 2 minutes or until cheese is melted. Garnish with cilantro.

Herb-Roasted Dijon Lamb and Vegetables

MAKES 6 SERVINGS

20 cloves garlic, peeled (about 2 medium heads)

¼ cup Dijon mustard

2 tablespoons water

2 tablespoons fresh rosemary leaves

1 tablespoon fresh thyme

1¼ teaspoons salt, divided

1 teaspoon black pepper

4½ pounds boneless leg of lamb, trimmed

1 pound parsnips, cut diagonally into ½-inch pieces

1 pound carrots, cut diagonally into ½-inch pieces

2 large onions, cut into ½-inch wedges

3 tablespoons extra virgin olive oil, divided

1. Combine garlic, mustard, water, rosemary, thyme, ¾ teaspoon salt and pepper in food processor; process until smooth. Spoon mixture over top and sides of lamb. Cover and refrigerate at least 8 hours.

2. Preheat oven to 500°F. Line baking sheet with foil; top with broiler rack. Spray rack with nonstick cooking spray. Combine parsnips, carrots, onions and 2 tablespoons oil in large bowl; toss to coat. Spread on broiler rack; top with lamb.

3. Roast 15 minutes. *Reduce oven temperature to 325°F.* Roast 1 hour 20 minutes or until lamb is 155°F for medium or to desired doneness.

4. Remove lamb to cutting board; tent with foil. Let stand 10 minutes before slicing. Continue roasting vegetables 10 minutes.

5. Transfer vegetables to large bowl. Add remaining 1 tablespoon oil and ½ teaspoon salt; toss to coat. Thinly slice lamb; serve with vegetables.

Roasted Salmon with New Potatoes and Red Onions

MAKES 6 SERVINGS

¼ cup chicken broth

1 tablespoon olive oil

1½ pounds small new potatoes, cut into halves

1 medium red onion, cut into ¼-inch wedges

6 salmon fillets (about 4 ounces each)

¾ teaspoon salt

½ teaspoon black pepper

Sprigs fresh tarragon or dill (optional)

1. Preheat oven to 400°F. Spray baking sheet with nonstick cooking spray.

2. Combine broth and oil in small bowl. Combine potatoes and half of broth mixture on prepared baking sheet; toss to coat.

3. Roast 20 minutes. Add onion and remaining broth mixture to baking sheet; toss to coat. Push vegetables to edges of baking sheet; place fish in center. Sprinkle fish and vegetables with salt and pepper. Roast 10 to 15 minutes or until center of fish is opaque and vegetables are tender. Garnish with tarragon.

Rosemary Pork Tenderloin and Vegetables

MAKES 6 SERVINGS

¼ cup chicken broth

1 tablespoon olive or vegetable oil

3 large parsnips, peeled and cut diagonally into ½-inch slices

2 cups baby carrots

1 red bell pepper, cut into ¾-inch pieces

1 medium onion, cut into wedges

2 small pork tenderloins (12 ounces each)

2 tablespoons Dijon or spicy Dijon mustard

2 teaspoons dried rosemary

¾ teaspoon salt

½ teaspoon black pepper

1. Preheat oven to 400°F. Spray baking sheet with nonstick cooking spray.

2. Combine broth and oil in small bowl. Combine parsnips, carrots and 3 tablespoons broth mixture on prepared baking sheet; toss to coat. Spread vegetables in single layer.

3. Roast vegetables 10 minutes. Add bell pepper, onion and remaining broth mixture to baking sheet; toss to coat. Push vegetables to edges of baking sheet. Place pork in center of baking sheet; spread with mustard. Sprinkle pork and vegetables with rosemary, salt and black pepper.

4. Roast 25 to 30 minutes or until vegetables are tender and pork is 145°F. Remove pork to cutting board; tent with foil. Let stand 5 minutes before slicing. Cut into ½-inch slices; serve with vegetables and any juices from pan.

Chorizo Artichoke Kabobs with Mustard Vinaigrette

MAKES 2 SERVINGS

1 can (about 14 ounces) large artichoke hearts, drained

2 fully cooked chorizo-flavored chicken sausages or andouille sausages (3 ounces each)

3 tablespoons olive oil

2 teaspoons white wine vinegar

1 teaspoon Dijon mustard

Salt and black pepper

1. Preheat broiler. Soak six wooden skewers in water 20 minutes. Line baking sheet with heavy-duty foil.

2. Cut artichoke hearts in half. Cut each sausage diagonally into 6 slices. Arrange 2 artichoke pieces and 2 sausage slices on each skewer. Place skewers on prepared baking sheet.

3. Broil 4 inches from heat 4 minutes or until artichokes are hot and sausage is browned.

4. Meanwhile, whisk oil, vinegar and mustard in small bowl. until blended. Season with salt and pepper. Serve with kabobs.

Rosemary Parmesan Chicken Flatbread

MAKES 6 SERVINGS

1 package (about 14 ounces) refrigerated pizza dough

2 tablespoons sun-dried tomato vinaigrette dressing*

2 plum tomatoes, thinly sliced

1¼ cups shredded cooked chicken breast (4 ounces)

1½ to 2 cups baby spinach leaves, coarsely chopped

¼ cup grated Parmesan cheese

1 tablespoon minced fresh rosemary

If unavailable, substitute balsamic or red wine vinaigrette.

1. Preheat oven to 400°F. Spray baking sheet with nonstick cooking spray. Unroll dough on baking sheet.

2. Bake 5 minutes. Remove from oven; brush evenly with dressing. Layer with tomatoes, chicken, spinach and cheese. Sprinkle with rosemary.

3. Bake 8 to 10 minutes or until crust is golden brown. Cut into 12 slices.

Tilapia and Corn Baked in Parchment

MAKES 2 SERVINGS

⅔ cup fresh or frozen corn kernels

¼ cup finely chopped onion

¼ cup finely chopped red bell pepper

2 cloves garlic, minced

1 teaspoon chopped fresh rosemary leaves *or* ½ teaspoon dried rosemary, divided

½ teaspoon salt, divided

¼ teaspoon black pepper, divided

2 tilapia fillets (4 ounces each)

2 teaspoons olive oil

1. Preheat oven to 400°F. Cut two 15-inch squares of parchment paper; fold each piece in half.

2. Combine corn, onion, bell pepper, garlic, ½ teaspoon fresh rosemary, ¼ teaspoon salt and ⅛ teaspoon black pepper in small bowl; mix well. Open parchment paper; spoon half of corn mixture on one side of each piece, spreading out slightly.

3. Arrange tilapia fillets on top of corn mixture. Brush fish with oil; sprinkle with remaining ½ teaspoon fresh rosemary, ¼ teaspoon salt and ⅛ teaspoon black pepper.

4. To seal packets, fold top half of parchment over fish and corn. Fold and crimp along edges until completely sealed. Place packets on baking sheet.

5. Bake 15 minutes or until center of fish is opaque. Remove packets to serving plates; carefully cut centers of packets and peel back paper.

NOTE

Heavy-duty foil can be substituted for the parchment paper. To serve, remove fish and corn from foil.

Jalapeño-Lime Chicken

MAKES 8 SERVINGS

3 tablespoons jalapeño jelly

1 tablespoon olive oil

1 tablespoon lime juice

1 clove garlic, minced

1 teaspoon chili powder

½ teaspoon black pepper

⅛ teaspoon salt

8 bone-in chicken thighs

1. Preheat oven to 400°F. Line baking sheet with foil; spray foil with nonstick cooking spray.

2. Combine jelly, oil, lime juice, garlic, chili powder, pepper and salt in small bowl; mix well.

3. Arrange chicken on prepared baking sheet.

4. Bake 15 minutes; drain off juices. Turn chicken; brush with half of jelly mixture. Bake 20 minutes. Turn chicken; brush with remaining jelly mixture. Bake 10 to 15 minutes or until cooked through (165°F).

Beef Tenderloin with Roasted Vegetables

MAKES 10 SERVINGS

1 beef tenderloin (about 3 pounds), trimmed

½ cup chardonnay or other dry white wine

½ cup soy sauce

2 cloves garlic, sliced

1 tablespoon fresh rosemary leaves

1 tablespoon Dijon mustard

1 teaspoon dry mustard

1 pound small red or white potatoes, cut into 1-inch pieces

1 pound brussels sprouts

1 package (12 ounces) baby carrots

1. Place beef in large resealable food storage bag. Combine wine, soy sauce, garlic, rosemary, Dijon mustard and dry mustard in small bowl; mix well. Pour over beef. Seal bag; turn to coat. Marinate in refrigerator 4 to 12 hours, turning several times.

2. Preheat oven to 425°F. Spray baking sheet with nonstick cooking spray. Combine potatoes, brussels sprouts and carrots on baking sheet. Remove beef from marinade. Pour marinade over vegetables; toss to coat. Cover with foil.

3. Roast vegetables 30 minutes. Stir vegetables; place beef on top. Roast, uncovered, 35 to 45 minutes or until beef is 135°F for medium rare or until desired doneness. Remove beef to cutting board; tent with foil. Let stand 10 to 15 minutes before slicing. (Internal temperature will continue to rise 5° to 10°F during stand time.) Reserve drippings from pan to make gravy, if desired.

4. Stir vegetables; continue roasting if not tender. Slice beef; serve with roasted vegetables.

Pepperoni-Oregano Focaccia

MAKES 12 SERVINGS

1 tablespoon cornmeal

1 package (about 14 ounces) refrigerated pizza dough

½ cup finely chopped pepperoni (about 3 ounces)

1½ teaspoons finely chopped fresh oregano *or* ½ teaspoon dried oregano

2 teaspoons olive oil

1. Preheat oven to 425°F. Spray baking sheet with nonstick cooking spray; sprinkle with cornmeal.

2. Unroll dough on lightly floured surface; pat into 12×9-inch rectangle. Sprinkle half of pepperoni and half of oregano over one side of dough. Fold over dough, making 12×4½-inch rectangle.

3. Roll dough into 12×9-inch rectangle. Place on prepared baking sheet; prick dough with fork at 2-inch intervals (about 30 times). Brush with oil; sprinkle with remaining pepperoni and oregano.

4. Bake 12 to 15 minutes or until golden brown. (Prick dough several more times if it puffs as it bakes.) Cut into strips.

SLOW COOKER

Hearty Vegetarian Mac and Cheese

MAKES 6 SERVINGS

1 can (about 14 ounces) stewed tomatoes, undrained

1½ cups prepared Alfredo sauce

1½ cups (6 ounces) shredded mozzarella cheese, divided

8 ounces uncooked whole grain pasta (medium shells or penne), cooked until al dente

7 ounces Italian-flavored vegetarian sausage links, cut into ¼-inch slices

¾ cup fresh basil leaves, thinly sliced, divided

½ cup vegetable broth

½ teaspoon salt

2 tablespoons grated Parmesan cheese

1. Spray slow cooker with nonstick cooking spray. Combine tomatoes, Alfredo sauce, 1 cup mozzarella, pasta, sausage, ½ cup basil, broth and salt in slow cooker; mix well. Top with remaining ½ cup mozzarella and Parmesan.

2. Cover; cook on LOW 3½ hours or on HIGH 2 hours. Top with remaining ¼ cup basil.

Braised Short Ribs with Sweet Potatoes

MAKES 4 SERVINGS

1 tablespoon olive oil

3 pounds bone-in beef short ribs, trimmed

1 teaspoon ground cumin, divided

1 teaspoon salt

½ teaspoon black pepper

2 medium onions, halved and thinly sliced

10 cloves garlic, thinly sliced

2 tablespoons balsamic vinegar

2 tablespoons honey

1 whole cinnamon stick

2 whole star anise pods

2 large sweet potatoes, peeled and cut into ¾-inch pieces

1 cup beef broth

1. Heat oil in large skillet over medium-high heat. Season ribs with ½ teaspoon cumin, salt and pepper. Add to skillet; cook 8 minutes or until browned, turning occasionally. Remove to plate.

2. Add onions and garlic to skillet; cook over medium heat 12 to 14 minutes or until onions are lightly browned. Stir in vinegar; cook 1 minute. Add remaining ½ teaspoon cumin, honey, cinnamon stick and star anise; cook and stir 30 seconds. Transfer mixture to slow cooker. Stir in sweet potatoes; top with ribs. Pour in broth.

3. Cover; cook on LOW 8 to 9 hours or until meat is falling off the bones. Remove and discard bones, cinnamon stick and star anise. Turn off heat; let stand 5 to 10 minutes. Skim off fat before serving.

Pork and Tomato Ragoût

MAKES 6 SERVINGS

2 pounds cubed pork stew meat

¼ cup all-purpose flour

3 tablespoons vegetable oil

1¼ cups dry white wine

2 pounds unpeeled red potatoes, cut into ½-inch pieces

1 can (about 14 ounces) diced tomatoes

1 cup finely chopped onion

1 cup water

½ cup finely chopped celery

2 cloves garlic, minced

½ teaspoon black pepper

1 cinnamon stick

3 tablespoons chopped fresh parsley

1. Combine pork and flour in large bowl; toss to coat. Heat oil in large skillet over medium-high heat. Add pork; cook until browned. Transfer to slow cooker.

2. Add wine to skillet; bring to a boil, scraping up browned bits from bottom of skillet. Pour into slow cooker. Add potatoes, tomatoes, onion, water, celery, garlic, pepper and cinnamon stick.

3. Cover; cook on LOW 6 to 8 hours or until pork and potatoes are tender. Remove and discard cinnamon stick. Adjust seasonings, if desired. Sprinkle with parsley.

TIP

Vegetables such as potatoes and carrots can sometimes take longer to cook in a slow cooker than meat. Place cut vegetables along the side of the slow cooker when possible.

Rustic Italian White Bean Soup

MAKES 8 TO 10 SERVINGS

10 cups chicken broth

1 package (16 ounces) dried Great Northern beans, rinsed and sorted

1 can (about 14 ounces) diced tomatoes

1 large onion, chopped

3 carrots, chopped

6 ounces bacon, crisp-cooked and chopped

4 cloves garlic, minced

1 sprig fresh rosemary *or* 1 teaspoon dried rosemary

1 teaspoon black pepper

1. Combine broth, beans, tomatoes, onion, carrots, bacon, garlic, rosemary and pepper in slow cooker.

2. Cover; cook on LOW 8 hours. Remove and discard rosemary before serving.

SERVING SUGGESTION

Place slices of toasted Italian bread in soup bowls; drizzle with olive oil. Ladle soup over bread.

Greek-Style Meatballs and Spinach

MAKES 4 SERVINGS

½ cup old-fashioned oats

¼ cup minced onion

1 clove garlic, minced

¼ teaspoon dried oregano

⅛ teaspoon black pepper

1 egg, lightly beaten

8 ounces ground lamb

1 cup beef broth

½ teaspoon salt

½ cup plain yogurt

1 teaspoon all-purpose flour

4 cups baby spinach, coarsely chopped

3 cups hot cooked egg noodles

1. Combine oats, onion, garlic, oregano and pepper in medium bowl; mix well. Stir in egg. Add lamb; mix gently. Shape mixture into 16 balls; place in slow cooker. Add broth and salt.

2. Cover; cook on LOW 6 hours. Whisk yogurt and flour in small bowl until blended. Whisk about ¼ cup hot liquid from slow cooker into yogurt mixture. Stir yogurt mixture into liquid in slow cooker. Add spinach.

3. Cover; cook on LOW 10 minutes or until heated through. Serve over noodles.

New England Pot Roast

MAKES 6 TO 8 SERVINGS

1 beef chuck pot roast (about 2½ pounds), trimmed and cut into bite-size pieces

Salt and black pepper

3 unpeeled medium baking potatoes (about 1 pound), cut into quarters

2 large carrots, cut into ¾-inch slices

2 stalks celery, cut into ¾-inch slices

1 medium onion, sliced

1 large parsnip, cut into ¾-inch slices

2 bay leaves

1 teaspoon dried rosemary

½ teaspoon dried thyme

½ cup beef broth

1. Season beef with salt and pepper. Combine potatoes, carrots, celery, onion, parsnip, bay leaves, rosemary and thyme in slow cooker. Place beef over vegetables. Pour broth over beef.

2. Cover; cook on LOW 8½ to 9 hours or until beef is fork-tender. Remove beef and vegetables to serving platter. Remove and discard bay leaves.

TIP

To make gravy, pour cooking liquid into 2-cup measure; let stand 5 minutes. Skim off fat. Bring cooking liquid to a boil in small saucepan over medium-high heat. For each cup, stir ¼ cup cold water into 2 tablespoons all-purpose flour in small bowl until smooth. Add flour mixture to boiling cooking liquid; cook and stir 1 minute or until thickened.

Sweet and Sour Chicken

MAKES 4 SERVINGS

¼ cup chicken broth

2 tablespoons
soy sauce

2 tablespoons
hoisin sauce

1 tablespoon
cider vinegar

1 tablespoon
tomato paste

2 teaspoons packed
brown sugar

1 clove garlic, minced

¼ teaspoon black
pepper

1 pound boneless
skinless chicken
thighs, cut into
1-inch pieces

2 teaspoons cornstarch

2 tablespoons snipped
fresh chives

Hot cooked rice

1. Combine broth, soy sauce, hoisin sauce, vinegar, tomato paste, brown sugar, garlic and pepper in slow cooker; mix well. Add chicken; stir to coat.

2. Cover; cook on LOW 2½ to 3½ hours. Remove chicken to bowl with slotted spoon; keep warm.

3. Whisk cornstarch into 2 tablespoons cooking liquid in small bowl until smooth. Add to slow cooker with chives. *Turn slow cooker to HIGH.* Cook, uncovered, 2 minutes or until sauce is slightly thickened, stirring constantly. Serve chicken and sauce over rice.

New Mexican Green Chile Pork Stew

MAKES 6 SERVINGS

1½ pounds boneless pork shoulder, cut into 1-inch pieces

2 medium baking potatoes or sweet potatoes, peeled and cut into 1-inch pieces

1 cup chopped onion

1 cup frozen corn

1 can (4 ounces) diced mild green chiles

1 jar (16 ounces) salsa verde (green salsa)

2 teaspoons sugar

2 teaspoons ground cumin or chili powder

1 teaspoon dried oregano

Hot cooked rice

¼ cup chopped fresh cilantro (optional)

1. Combine pork, potatoes, onion, corn and chiles in slow cooker. Combine salsa, sugar, cumin and oregano in small bowl; mix well. Pour over pork and vegetables; stir gently to coat.

2. Cover; cook on LOW 6 to 8 hours or on HIGH 4 to 5 hours or until pork is tender. Serve with rice; garnish with cilantro.

Chicken in Enchilada Sauce

MAKES 4 SERVINGS

1 can (about 14 ounces) diced tomatoes with green chiles

1 can (10 ounces) enchilada sauce

1 cup frozen or canned corn

¼ teaspoon ground cumin

¼ teaspoon red pepper flakes

⅛ teaspoon black pepper

1½ pounds boneless skinless chicken thighs, cut into bite-size pieces

2 tablespoons minced fresh cilantro

½ cup (2 ounces) shredded pepper jack cheese

Sliced green onions (optional)

1. Combine tomatoes, enchilada sauce, corn, cumin, red pepper flakes and black pepper in slow cooker. Add chicken; mix well.

2. Cover; cook on LOW 6 to 7 hours. Stir in cilantro. Sprinkle with cheese; garnish with green onions.

Barley and Sausage Gumbo

MAKES 4 SERVINGS

1 small onion, chopped

1 large green bell
   pepper, chopped

1 cup frozen sliced okra

1 medium stalk celery,
   chopped

1 clove garlic, minced

1 cup chicken broth

1 cup tomato purée

¼ cup uncooked
   pearled barley

1 teaspoon dried
   oregano

¾ teaspoon salt

⅛ teaspoon red pepper
   flakes

2 andouille sausages
   (3 ounces each),
   cut into ½-inch
   slices

1. Combine onion, bell pepper, okra, celery and garlic in slow cooker. Add broth, tomato purée, barley, oregano, salt and red pepper flakes; mix well. Stir in sausages.

2. Cover; cook on LOW 5 to 6 hours. Let stand 5 minutes before serving.

Turkey Noodle Soup

MAKES 8 SERVINGS

2 turkey drumsticks
   (about 1¾ pounds)

3 carrots, sliced

3 stalks celery,
   thinly sliced

1 onion, chopped

2 cloves garlic, minced

1 teaspoon poultry
   seasoning

4 cups chicken broth

3 cups water

8 ounces uncooked
   egg noodles

⅓ cup chopped fresh
   Italian parsley

   Salt and black pepper

1. Combine turkey, carrots, celery, onion, garlic and poultry seasoning in slow cooker. Pour broth and water over top.

2. Cover; cook on HIGH 5 hours or until meat is falling off the bones. Remove turkey to plate. Add noodles to slow cooker. Cover; cook on HIGH 30 minutes or until tender.

3. Meanwhile, cut turkey into bite-size pieces; discard skin and bones. Return turkey to slow cooker. Cover; cook on HIGH until heated through. Stir in parsley; season with salt and pepper.

Sweet and Savory Brisket

MAKES 8 SERVINGS

1 large onion,
   thinly sliced

1 beef brisket
   (2 to 2½ pounds),
   trimmed

   Salt and black pepper

⅔ cup chili sauce,
   divided

1½ tablespoons packed
   brown sugar

¼ teaspoon ground
   cinnamon

2 large sweet potatoes,
   cut into 1-inch
   pieces

1 cup (5 ounces)
   pitted prunes

2 tablespoons
   cold water

2 tablespoons
   cornstarch

1. Place onion in slow cooker; top with brisket. Sprinkle with salt and pepper; top with ⅓ cup chili sauce. Cover; cook on HIGH 3½ hours.

2. Combine remaining ⅓ cup chili sauce, brown sugar and cinnamon in large bowl; mix well. Add sweet potatoes and prunes; toss to coat. Spoon mixture over brisket. Cover; cook on HIGH 1¼ to 1½ hours.

3. Remove brisket to large cutting board. Tent with foil; let stand 10 to 15 minutes before slicing. Remove sweet potato mixture to large serving platter with slotted spoon; cover to keep warm.

4. Stir water into cornstarch in small bowl until smooth; whisk into cooking liquid. Cover; cook on HIGH 10 to 15 minutes or until sauce is thickened. Slice brisket; serve with sweet potato mixture and sauce.

Hearty Chicken Chili

MAKES 6 SERVINGS

1 onion, finely chopped

1 jalapeño pepper,
    minced

1 clove garlic, minced

1½ teaspoons chili
    powder

¾ teaspoon salt

½ teaspoon ground
    cumin

½ teaspoon dried
    oregano

½ teaspoon black
    pepper

¼ teaspoon red pepper
    flakes (optional)

1½ pounds boneless
    skinless chicken
    thighs, cut into
    1-inch pieces

2 cans (about 15 ounces
    each) hominy,
    rinsed and drained

1 can (about 15 ounces)
    pinto beans, rinsed
    and drained

1 cup chicken broth

1 tablespoon all-
    purpose flour
    (optional)

   Chopped fresh
    cilantro (optional)

1. Combine onion, jalapeño pepper, garlic, chili powder, salt, cumin, oregano, black pepper and red pepper flakes, if desired, in slow cooker; mix well. Stir in chicken, hominy, beans and broth until blended.

2. Cover; cook on LOW 7 hours.

3. For thicker chili, stir 1 tablespoon flour into 3 tablespoons cooking liquid in small bowl until smooth. Stir into slow cooker. *Turn slow cooker to HIGH.* Cover; cook 10 minutes or until thickened. Garnish with parsley.

Chorizo Burritos

MAKES 4 SERVINGS

15 ounces Mexican chorizo sausage, cut into bite-size pieces

1 can (about 15 ounces) red beans, rinsed and drained

1 can (about 14 ounces) diced tomatoes

1 can (11 ounces) corn, drained

2 green or red bell peppers, cut into 1-inch pieces

1 cup chicken broth

½ teaspoon ground cumin

½ teaspoon ground cinnamon

8 (8-inch) flour tortillas, warmed

2 cups hot cooked rice

Shredded Monterey Jack cheese

1. Combine chorizo, beans, tomatoes, corn, bell peppers, broth, cumin and cinnamon in slow cooker; mix well.

2. Cover; cook on LOW 6 to 8 hours.

3. Spoon chorizo filling down centers of warm tortillas; top with rice and shredded cheese. Roll up tortillas and filling; serve immediately.

Middle Eastern Beef and Eggplant Stew

MAKES 4 SERVINGS

1 tablespoon olive oil

1 small eggplant, trimmed and cut into 1-inch pieces

2 cups shiitake or cremini mushrooms, quartered

1 can (about 14 ounces) diced tomatoes

8 ounces boneless beef top round steak, cut into 1-inch pieces

1 medium onion, chopped

1 cup beef broth

1 clove garlic, minced

1 teaspoon salt

½ teaspoon ground cumin

¼ teaspoon red pepper flakes

¼ teaspoon ground cinnamon

Grated peel of 1 lemon

⅛ teaspoon black pepper

1. Heat oil in large skillet over medium-high heat. Add eggplant; cook and stir 3 to 5 minutes or until lightly browned. Transfer to slow cooker.

2. Stir in mushrooms, tomatoes, beef, onion, broth, garlic, salt, cumin, red pepper flakes, cinnamon, lemon peel and black pepper; mix well.

3. Cover; cook on LOW 6 hours.

PRESSURE COOKER

Mu Shu Turkey

MAKES 6 SERVINGS

1 jar (about 7 ounces) plum sauce, divided

¼ cup orange juice (juice of 1 medium orange)

¼ cup finely chopped onion

1 tablespoon minced fresh ginger

¼ teaspoon salt

¼ teaspoon ground cinnamon

1 pound boneless turkey breast, cut into thin strips

6 (7-inch) flour tortillas

3 cups coleslaw mix

1. Combine ⅓ cup plum sauce, orange juice, onion, ginger, salt and cinnamon in pot; mix well. Add turkey, stir to coat.

2. Secure lid and move pressure release valve to sealing or locked position. Cook at high pressure 4 minutes.

3. When cooking is complete, press Cancel and use quick release.

4. Press Sauté; cook 2 to 3 minutes or until sauce is reduced and thickens slightly.

5. Spread remaining jarred plum sauce over tortillas; top with turkey and coleslaw mix. Fold bottom edge of tortillas over filling; fold in sides and roll up to completely enclose filling. Serve with remaining cooking sauce for dipping.

Chicken Tortilla Soup

MAKES 4 TO 6 SERVINGS

2 cans (about 14 ounces each) diced tomatoes

1½ pounds boneless skinless chicken thighs

1 onion, chopped

½ cup chicken broth

1 can (4 ounces) diced green chiles

2 cloves garlic, minced

1 teaspoon salt

1 teaspoon ground cumin

¼ teaspoon black pepper

4 corn tortillas, cut into ¼-inch strips

2 tablespoons chopped fresh cilantro

½ cup (2 ounces) shredded Monterey Jack cheese

1 avocado, diced and tossed with lime juice

Lime wedges

1. Combine tomatoes, chicken, onion, broth, chiles, garlic, salt, cumin and pepper in pot; mix well.

2. Secure lid and move pressure release valve to sealing or locked position. Cook at high pressure 9 minutes.

3. When cooking is complete, use natural release for 10 minutes, then release remaining pressure.

4. Remove chicken to plate; shred into bite-size pieces when cool enough to handle. Stir into soup.

5. Press Sauté; add tortillas and cilantro to soup. Cook and stir 2 minutes or until heated through. Top with cheese, avocado and squeeze of lime juice. Serve immediately.

Classic Beef Stew

MAKES 8 SERVINGS

2½ **pounds cubed beef stew meat**

¼ **cup all-purpose flour**

1½ **teaspoons salt, divided**

2 **tablespoons olive oil, divided**

1 **cup beef broth**

1 **medium onion, chopped**

1 **ounce dried oyster mushrooms, chopped**

2 **teaspoons garlic powder**

1 **teaspoon dried basil**

1 **teaspoon dried oregano**

½ **teaspoon dried rosemary**

½ **teaspoon dried marjoram**

½ **teaspoon dried sage**

½ **teaspoon dried thyme**

8 **fingerling potatoes, halved lengthwise**

1 **cup baby carrots**

Black pepper

Chopped fresh Italian parsley (optional)

1 Combine beef, flour and ½ teaspoon salt in large resealable food storage bag; toss to coat. Press Sauté; heat 1 tablespoon oil in pot. Add half of beef; cook about 5 minutes or until browned. Remove to plate; repeat with remaining oil and beef.

2. Add broth, onion, mushrooms, garlic powder, remaining 1 teaspoon salt, basil, oregano, rosemary, marjoram, sage and thyme to pot; mix well. Secure lid and move pressure release valve to sealing or locked position. Cook at high pressure 30 minutes.

3. When cooking is complete, press Cancel and use quick release.

4. Add potatoes and carrots to pot. Secure lid and move pressure release valve to sealing or locked position. Cook at high pressure 10 minutes.

5. When cooking is complete, press Cancel and use quick release. Season with additional salt and pepper, if desired. Garnish with parsley.

Sweet Potato and Black Bean Chili

MAKES 6 SERVINGS

1 tablespoon olive oil

1 large onion, chopped

4 teaspoons chili powder

2 cloves garlic, minced

1 teaspoon salt

1 teaspoon chipotle chili powder

½ teaspoon ground cumin

2 cans (about 15 ounces each) black beans, rinsed and drained

1 large sweet potato, peeled and cut into ½-inch pieces

1 can (about 14 ounces) diced tomatoes

1 can (about 14 ounces) crushed tomatoes

1½ cups vegetable broth or water

Optional toppings: sour cream, sliced green onions, shredded Cheddar cheese and/or tortilla chips

1. Press Sauté; heat oil in pot. Add onion; cook and stir 3 minutes or until softened. Add chili powder, garlic, salt, chipotle chili powder and cumin; cook and stir 1 minute. Stir in beans, sweet potato, diced tomatoes, crushed tomatoes and broth; mix well.

2. Secure lid and move pressure release valve to sealing or locked position. Cook at high pressure 4 minutes.

3. When cooking is complete, press Cancel and use quick release.

4. Press Sauté; cook 3 to 5 minutes or until chili thickens to desired consistency, stirring frequently. Serve with desired toppings.

Hot and Sweet Sausage Sandwiches

MAKES 5 SERVINGS

1½ cups pasta sauce

1 large sweet onion, cut into ¼-inch slices

1 medium green bell pepper, cut into ½-inch slices

1 medium red bell pepper, cut into ½-inch slices

1½ tablespoons packed dark brown sugar

1 package (16 ounces) hot Italian sausage links (5 sausages)

5 Italian rolls, split

1. Combine pasta sauce, onion, bell peppers and brown sugar in pot; mix well. Add sausages to pot; spoon some of sauce mixture over sausages.

2. Secure lid and move pressure release valve to sealing or locked position. Cook at high pressure 5 minutes.

3. When cooking is complete, use natural release for 10 minutes, then release remaining pressure. Remove sausages to plate; tent with foil.

4. Press Sauté; cook 10 minutes or until sauce is reduced by one third, stirring occasionally. Serve sausages in rolls; top with sauce.

TIP

If you have leftover sauce, refrigerate or freeze it and serve over pasta or polenta. Top with grated Parmesan cheese.

Mushroom Barley Soup

MAKES 6 TO 8 SERVINGS

2 tablespoons olive oil

1 onion, chopped

2 carrots, chopped

2 stalks celery, chopped

3 cloves garlic, minced

1 teaspoon salt

½ teaspoon dried thyme

½ teaspoon black pepper

5 cups vegetable or chicken broth

1 package (16 ounces) sliced mushrooms

½ cup uncooked pearl barley

½ ounce dried porcini or shiitake mushrooms

1. Press Sauté; heat oil in pot. Add onion, carrots and celery; cook and stir 5 minutes or until vegetables are softened. Add garlic, salt, thyme and pepper; cook and stir 1 minute. Stir in broth, sliced mushrooms, barley and dried mushrooms; mix well.

2. Secure lid and move pressure release valve to sealing or locked position. Cook at high pressure 22 minutes.

3. When cooking is complete, use natural release for 10 minutes, then release remaining pressure.

Turkey Ropa Vieja

MAKES 4 SERVINGS

1 tablespoon olive oil

1 onion, thinly sliced

1 green bell pepper, chopped

1 clove garlic, minced

¾ teaspoon ground cumin

½ teaspoon dried oregano

2 medium tomatoes, chopped

1 can (8 ounces) tomato sauce

⅓ cup sliced pimiento-stuffed green olives

½ teaspoon salt

¼ teaspoon black pepper

1 pound turkey tenderloins (2 large or 3 small) *or* 1½ pounds boneless turkey breast, cut into 3 to 4 pieces

1 tablespoon lemon juice

Hot cooked rice and beans (optional)

1. Press Sauté; heat oil in pot. Add onion and bell pepper; cook and stir 3 minutes or until softened. Add garlic, cumin and oregano; cook and stir 30 seconds. Stir in tomatoes, tomato sauce, olives, salt and black pepper; mix well. Add turkey to pot, pressing into tomato mixture.

2. Secure lid and move pressure release valve to sealing or locked position. Cook at high pressure 20 minutes.

3. When cooking is complete, use natural release for 10 minutes, then release remaining pressure. Remove turkey to plate.

4. Press Sauté; cook 10 to 15 minutes or until sauce is reduced by one third.

5. Meanwhile, shred turkey into bite-size pieces when cool enough to handle. Add shredded turkey and lemon juice to sauce; mix well. Serve with rice and beans, if desired.

Beef Pot Roast Dinner

MAKES 4 TO 6 SERVINGS

2 cloves garlic, minced

1 teaspoon salt

1 teaspoon herbes
    de Provence*

1 teaspoon ground sage

1 teaspoon ground
    cumin

1 teaspoon black pepper

1 beef eye of round
    roast (about
    2½ pounds),
    trimmed

2 tablespoons olive oil

1 cup beef broth

4 small turnips, peeled
    and cut into
    wedges

12 medium fresh brussels
    sprouts, trimmed

2 cups halved small
    new red potatoes

2 cups baby carrots

1 cup pearl onions,
    skins removed *or*
    1 large onion, cut
    into wedges

*Or substitute ¼ teaspoon
each dried rosemary,
thyme, sage and savory.*

1. Combine garlic, salt, herbes de Provence, sage, cumin and pepper in small bowl; mix well. Rub mixture into all sides of beef.

2. Press Sauté; heat oil in pot. Add beef; cook about 5 minutes or until browned on all sides. Remove to plate. Stir in broth, scraping up browned bits from bottom of pot. Place rack in pot; place beef on rack.

3. Secure lid and move pressure release valve to sealing or locked position. Cook at high pressure 50 minutes.

4. When cooking is complete, use natural release for 5 minutes, then release remaining pressure.

5. Add turnips, brussels sprouts, potatoes, carrots and onion to pot. Secure lid and move pressure release valve to sealing or locked position. Cook at high pressure 10 minutes.

6. When cooking is complete, press Cancel and use quick release. Serve beef and vegetables with cooking liquid or thicken sauce, if desired.

Spicy Squash and Chicken Soup

MAKES 4 SERVINGS

1 tablespoon vegetable oil

1 small onion, finely chopped

1 stalk celery, finely chopped

2 cups chicken broth

2 cups cubed butternut squash (1-inch pieces)

1 can (about 14 ounces) diced tomatoes with chiles

8 ounces boneless skinless chicken thighs, cut into ½-inch pieces

½ teaspoon salt

½ teaspoon ground ginger

⅛ teaspoon ground cumin

⅛ teaspoon black pepper

2 teaspoons lime juice

½ to 1 teaspoon hot pepper sauce

Fresh cilantro or parsley sprigs (optional)

1. Press Sauté; heat oil in pot. Add onion and celery; cook and stir 4 minutes or until vegetables are softened. Add broth, squash, tomatoes, chicken, salt, ginger, cumin and black pepper; mix well.

2. Secure lid and move pressure release valve to sealing or locked position. Cook at high pressure 5 minutes.

3. When cooking is complete, use natural release for 10 minutes, then release remaining pressure.

4. Stir in lime juice and hot pepper sauce; garnish with cilantro.

Shortcut Bolognese

MAKES 4 SERVINGS

1 tablespoon olive oil

1 pound ground beef

1 medium onion,
    chopped

½ small carrot,
    finely chopped

½ stalk celery,
    finely chopped

3 tablespoons
    tomato paste

1 cup dry white wine

½ cup milk

⅛ teaspoon ground
    nutmeg

1 can (about 14 ounces)
    whole tomatoes,
    coarsely chopped,
    juice reserved

½ cup beef broth

1 teaspoon salt

1 teaspoon dried basil

½ teaspoon dried thyme

⅛ teaspoon black
    pepper

1 bay leaf

Hot cooked spaghetti

Grated Parmesan
    cheese (optional)

1. Press Sauté; heat oil in pot. Add beef; cook about 8 minutes or until all liquid evaporates, stirring to break up meat. Drain fat.

2. Add onion, carrot and celery to pot; cook and stir 4 minutes. Add tomato paste; cook and stir 2 minutes. Add wine; cook about 5 minutes or until wine has almost evaporated. Add milk and nutmeg; cook and stir 3 to 4 minutes or until milk has almost evaporated. Stir in tomatoes with juice, broth, salt, basil, thyme, pepper and bay leaf; mix well.

3. Secure lid and move pressure release valve to sealing or locked position. Cook at high pressure 18 minutes.

4. When cooking is complete, press Cancel and use quick release. Remove and discard bay leaf. Serve sauce with spaghetti; top with cheese, if desired.

Shakshuka

MAKES 4 SERVINGS

2 tablespoons extra virgin olive oil

1 large red bell pepper, chopped

1 medium onion, chopped

3 cloves garlic, minced

2 teaspoons sugar

2 teaspoons ground cumin

1 teaspoon paprika

1 teaspoon chili powder

½ teaspoon salt

¼ teaspoon red pepper flakes

1 can (28 ounces) crushed tomatoes

¾ cup crumbled feta cheese

4 eggs

1. Press Sauté; heat oil in pot. Add bell pepper and onion; cook and stir 3 minutes or until softened. Add garlic, sugar, cumin, paprika, chili powder, salt and red pepper flakes to pot; cook and stir 1 minute. Stir in tomatoes; mix well.

2. Secure lid and move pressure release valve to sealing or locked position. Cook at high pressure 10 minutes.

3. When cooking is complete, press Cancel and use quick release.

4. Stir in cheese. Make four wells in sauce for eggs, leaving space between each. Slide eggs, one at a time, into wells in sauce. (For best results, crack each egg into small bowl before sliding into sauce.)

5. Secure lid and move pressure release valve to sealing or locked position. Cook at low pressure 1 minute. When cooking is complete, press Cancel and use quick release. To cook eggs longer, press Sauté and cook until desired doneness.

Turkey Stroganoff

MAKES 4 SERVINGS

1 tablespoon olive oil

4 cups sliced
    mushrooms

2 stalks celery, sliced

2 medium shallots *or*
    ½ small onion,
    minced

2 turkey tenderloins
    (about 5 ounces
    each), cut into
    1-inch pieces

¼ cup chicken broth

1½ tablespoons
    Worcestershire
    sauce

¾ teaspoon salt

½ teaspoon dried thyme

¼ teaspoon black
    pepper

½ cup sour cream

1 tablespoon
    all-purpose flour

    Hot cooked egg
    noodles

1. Press Sauté; heat oil in pot. Add mushrooms, celery and shallots; cook and stir 5 minutes or until vegetables are tender. Add turkey, broth, Worcestershire sauce, salt, thyme and pepper; mix well.

2. Secure lid and move pressure release valve to sealing or locked position. Cook at high pressure 6 minutes.

3. When cooking is complete, use natural release for 5 minutes, then release remaining pressure.

4. Combine sour cream and flour in small bowl; stir in ¼ cup hot cooking liquid from pot until smooth. Press Sauté; add sour cream mixture to pot. Cook and stir 3 minutes or until sauce thickens. Serve over noodles.

Mole Chili

MAKES 4 SERVINGS

2 tablespoons olive oil, divided

1½ pounds boneless beef chuck, cut into 1-inch pieces

2 medium onions, chopped

5 cloves garlic, minced

1 cup beef broth, divided

1 can (about 14 ounces) fire-roasted diced tomatoes

2 corn tortillas, each cut into 4 wedges

2 tablespoons chili powder

1 tablespoon ancho chili powder

1 teaspoon dried oregano

1 teaspoon ground cumin

¾ teaspoon salt

¾ teaspoon ground cinnamon

½ teaspoon black pepper

1 can (about 15 ounces) red kidney beans, rinsed and drained

1½ ounces semisweet chocolate, chopped

1. Press Sauté; heat 1 tablespoon oil in pot. Add beef in two batches; cook about 5 minutes or until browned. Remove to plate. Add remaining 1 tablespoon oil, onions and garlic to pot; cook and stir about 3 minutes or until softened. Stir in ½ cup broth, scraping up browned bits from bottom of pot. Stir in remaining ½ cup broth, beef, tomatoes, tortillas, chili powders, oregano, cumin, salt, cinnamon and pepper; mix well.

2. Secure lid and move pressure release valve to sealing or locked position. Cook at high pressure 30 minutes.

3. When cooking is complete, use natural release for 15 minutes, then release remaining pressure.

4. Press Sauté; add beans and chocolate to pot. Cook and stir 2 minutes or until chocolate is melted and beans are heated through.

Split Pea Soup

MAKES 4 TO 6 SERVINGS

8 slices bacon, chopped

1 onion, chopped

2 carrots, chopped

1 stalk celery, chopped

1 clove garlic, minced

½ teaspoon dried thyme

1 container (32 ounces) chicken broth

2 cups water

1 package (16 ounces) dried split peas, rinsed and sorted

¾ teaspoon salt

½ teaspoon black pepper

1 bay leaf

1. Press Sauté; cook and stir bacon in pot until crisp. Remove to paper towel-lined plate. Drain off all but 1 tablespoon drippings.

2. Add onion, carrots and celery to pot; cook and stir 5 minutes or until vegetables are softened. Add garlic and thyme; cook and stir 1 minute. Stir in broth and water, scraping up browned bits from bottom of pot. Add split peas, half of bacon, salt, pepper and bay leaf; mix well.

3. Secure lid and move pressure release valve to sealing or locked position. Cook at high pressure 8 minutes.

4. When cooking is complete, use natural release for 10 minutes, then release remaining pressure. Stir soup; remove and discard bay leaf. Garnish with remaining bacon.

NOTE

The soup may seem thin immediately after cooking, but it will thicken upon standing. If prepared in advance and refrigerated, thin the soup with water when reheating until the desired consistency is reached.

Shredded Beef Fajitas

MAKES 6 SERVINGS

1 beef flank steak (about 1 pound), cut into 2 pieces

¼ teaspoon salt

⅛ teaspoon black pepper

1 tablespoon vegetable oil

1 medium onion, chopped, divided

1 medium green bell pepper, cut into ½-inch pieces, divided

1 clove garlic, minced *or* ¼ teaspoon garlic powder

1 can (about 10 ounces) diced tomatoes with mild green chiles

½ package fajita seasoning mix (about 2 tablespoons)

6 (8-inch) flour tortillas, warmed

Optional toppings: sour cream, guacamole, shredded Cheddar cheese, salsa

1. Season beef with salt and black pepper. Press Sauté; heat oil in pot. Add beef; cook 3 to 4 minutes per side or until browned. Remove to plate. Add half of onion and half of bell pepper to pot; cook and stir 2 minutes. Add garlic; cook and stir 30 seconds. Add tomatoes and fajita seasoning mix; cook 2 minutes, scraping up browned bits from bottom of pot. Return beef to pot, pressing into liquid.

2. Secure lid and move pressure release valve to sealing or locked position. Cook at high pressure 23 minutes.

3. When cooking is complete, use natural release for 10 minutes, then release remaining pressure. Remove beef to clean plate; let stand 10 minutes.

4. Meanwhile, press Sauté; add remaining half of onion and bell pepper to pot. Cook about 8 minutes or until bell pepper is crisp-tender and liquid is reduced, stirring occasionally.

5. Shred beef into bite-size pieces. Return beef to pot; stir until blended. Serve beef mixture in tortillas with desired toppings.

METRIC CONVERSION CHART

VOLUME MEASUREMENTS (dry)

$^1/_8$ teaspoon = 0.5 mL
$^1/_4$ teaspoon = 1 mL
$^1/_2$ teaspoon = 2 mL
$^3/_4$ teaspoon = 4 mL
1 teaspoon = 5 mL
1 tablespoon = 15 mL
2 tablespoons = 30 mL
$^1/_4$ cup = 60 mL
$^1/_3$ cup = 75 mL
$^1/_2$ cup = 125 mL
$^2/_3$ cup = 150 mL
$^3/_4$ cup = 175 mL
1 cup = 250 mL
2 cups = 1 pint = 500 mL
3 cups = 750 mL
4 cups = 1 quart = 1 L

VOLUME MEASUREMENTS (fluid)

1 fluid ounce (2 tablespoons) = 30 mL
4 fluid ounces ($^1/_2$ cup) = 125 mL
8 fluid ounces (1 cup) = 250 mL
12 fluid ounces (1$^1/_2$ cups) = 375 mL
16 fluid ounces (2 cups) = 500 mL

WEIGHTS (mass)

$^1/_2$ ounce = 15 g
1 ounce = 30 g
3 ounces = 90 g
4 ounces = 120 g
8 ounces = 225 g
10 ounces = 285 g
12 ounces = 360 g
16 ounces = 1 pound = 450 g

DIMENSIONS

$^1/_{16}$ inch = 2 mm
$^1/_8$ inch = 3 mm
$^1/_4$ inch = 6 mm
$^1/_2$ inch = 1.5 cm
$^3/_4$ inch = 2 cm
1 inch = 2.5 cm

OVEN TEMPERATURES

250°F = 120°C
275°F = 140°C
300°F = 150°C
325°F = 160°C
350°F = 180°C
375°F = 190°C
400°F = 200°C
425°F = 220°C
450°F = 230°C

BAKING PAN SIZES

Utensil	Size in Inches/Quarts	Metric Volume	Size in Centimeters
Baking or	8×8×2	2 L	20×20×5
Cake Pan	9×9×2	2.5 L	23×23×5
(square or	12×8×2	3 L	30×20×5
rectangular)	13×9×2	3.5 L	33×23×5
Loaf Pan	8×4×3	1.5 L	20×10×7
	9×5×3	2 L	23×13×7
Round Layer	8×1½	1.2 L	20×4
Cake Pan	9×1½	1.5 L	23×4
Pie Plate	8×1¼	750 mL	20×3
	9×1¼	1 L	23×3
Baking Dish	1 quart	1 L	—
or Casserole	1½ quart	1.5 L	—
	2 quart	2 L	—